Harold Be Thy Name

Harold Be Thy Name

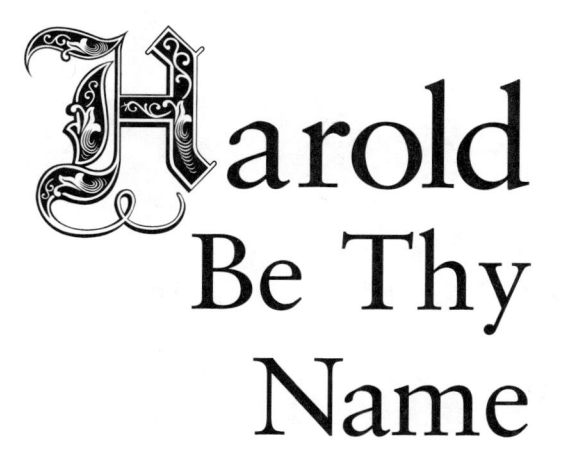

Lighthearted Daily Reflections
for People in Recovery

MALACHY MCCOURT

Carhil Ventures LLC

HAROLD BE THY NAME
Malachy McCourt

Copyright © 2004 by Malachy McCourt.
All rights reserved.

Library of Congress CIP data available from the publisher.

ISBN: 1-56649-296-3

Printed in the United States of America by
HAMILTON PRINTING COMPANY

Interior design and composition by
MULBERRY TREE PRESS, INC.
www.mulberrytreepress.com

First edition: January 2004

1   3   5   7   9   10   8   6   4   2

INTRODUCTION

by Malachy McCourt

JUST SUPPOSE that you found out that this day would be your last day alive on this earth, that you would die before midnight. Some of us would panic, screaming "NO! NO! NO!" Others would complain, "Why me?" Still others would travel as far away as possible, hoping that geographical distance would alter Death's mind, and another group might say, "Let me get ready, then, as there are some items I must take care of, and some arrangements to be made."

One nice thing about dying nowadays is you don't have to pack material supplies, like deodorants, toothpaste, aspirin, bathing suit, hairbrush, underwear, or outerwear—not a bloody thing. All you have to do is sit, and perhaps gather the family and friends for a farewell chat. Of course, before we do that, we ought to ring up or otherwise contact the various people we have slighted or injured in our lives and see if we can't make amends. Cleaning things up in this way does not mean seeking or expecting forgiveness, for sometimes injured parties will find that impossible to grant. But if you tell them you are about to die, you might elicit a "Bon voyage" at least. Your last day ought to be one of story, song, reminiscences, and loving embraces all round.

Good humor should prevail, and it would be advisable to avoid giving advice to those you are leaving—that is my advice. If you can think of any "Last words" that people might quote, such as "Before I die, I'd like to sing 'Ninety-nine Bottles of Beer on a Wall,'" you will be remembered as a grand deathbed wit.

Now, in America people do not die, and it's impolite even to mention the word *death,* particularly in the presence of undertakers (pardon me, funeral directors!), but it might divert your grieving gang if you could have charts and magic markers in your room to chronicle your journey into the beyond. Will you go up or down? Will it be cool, or extremely hot? Will you be likely to meet Mother Teresa, Adolf Hitler, Josef Stalin, Katharine Hepburn, St. Peter, Jesus, Moses, the Virgin Mary, Muhammad, Buddha, Francis of Assisi, Bill Wilson, Dr. Bob, your parents, God, people you dislike, etc.; and how long will it take to get to your final destination?

Now if you are not going to die today, it might be as well not to dwell on the event. Take my advice (I'm not using it myself): What you should do is assume you are going to live today, but give some thought to dying, thereby enjoying your last day. And any day you happen to be alive (which you will instantly recognize as you open your eyes), take a deep breath, open this book to the applicable page, leap out of bed (or fall out, if needs be), and LIVE the day as if it's to be your last. One day you will be right.

Now, just suppose again that it is NOT your day to die (death being the sort of thing that most people tend to procrastinate about, if at all possible), but, as Dr. Samuel Johnson once said, "Depend on it, sir! When a man knows he is to be hanged in a fortnight, it concentrates his mind wonderfully!" Keeping that in mind, let's see where we may possibly be at any given time whilst still alive. Some of us are:

Strolling
Playing
Traveling (on planes, trains, cars, buses, boats, ships)
Hospitalized
In a coma
Imprisoned
Institutionalized

All of us, however, are stuck in our own bodies. Now, the spirit keeps coming back to my body like a homing pigeon, because the bod aches, hungers, thirsts, needs evacuation, cleansing, and other daily cares. No matter where we go in that body, there we are: we go through life bestridden with warnings, advice, injunctions, prohibitions, admonitions, exhortations, threats, and caveats because there is the idea abroad that we are going to do the wrong thing because we have that body.

So, if we think of death as release, the spirit will be free to do all it wants and needs to do. The spirit is a permanent child, filled with wonder and a breathless excitement at the prospect of doing good. Whilst we have the body, we can capture that exhilaration every day of our lives and, as they say, "fake it 'til we make it." As Mark Twain put it, "In case of doubt, tell the truth," and I say, "In case of doubt, do the right thing." Not easy, but oh, so simple.

It's important to avoid killing yourself before you die. Take a dose of these words each day, instead of that first dram of whiskey, pint of brew, snifter of brandy, or gram of substance.

ACKNOWLEDGMENTS

My greatest affirmation is my friend/spouse, Diana.

Where would I be lurking if it were not for Charlie DeFanti and his constant encouragement?

Thanks to John Weber and his friend/spouse, Mara Lurie, for so many things.

To Robert Haydon Jones for officiating at these literary nuptials—thank you.

To Laurie Liss, for her good humor and good sense.

To my pal, sponsor, inspirer, and contributor, Bob Cranny—for all you are, thank you.

To my terrific children: To Siobhan, Malachy, Nina, Conor and Juliette, and Cormac, you are my loves.

To Lourdes, Stephanie, and Jazmin, for the song and the light in my day.

To Fiona, Mark, Adrianna, and Gillian, the grandest of grandchildren.

To my brothers, Frank, Alphie, and Mike—I cherish you.

To Mark Pollman, compiler of *Bottled Wisdom* (Weldstone Media), a man of spirit, genius, and great humor, for the best book on drink and drinking. Thank you.

To the men at Uncle John, L.A.

To the raucous men of Roxbury, L.A.

To Jack Zwaska and Mike Molloy—I'd be nowhere without you.

And to Bill W. and Dr. Bob, for the garden that beautified this world.

Harold
Be Thy Name

JANUARY 1

*"Our Father Who art in heaven.
Harold be Thy name."*
(The way I heard The Lord's Prayer as a child.)

I remember wondering why God had so named himself. It appeared it was also sort of a family name—in that there was a song about Harold Angels singing.

REFLECTION

We follow a 12-Step Program of Recovery.
Our 12th Step begins,

*"Having had a spiritual awakening
as the result of these steps . . ."*

The linchpin of our recovery is our reliance on our Higher Power. You hear many names for the Higher Power in the rooms, but the fact is, any name will do if it affirms the spiritual connection for us.

AFFIRMATION

Today, I will strive to stay close to my Higher Power and remember the answer to the question, "Who keeps us sober?"

January 2

> Why do we never "eat" to anyone's health, but always "drink" to it? Why should we not stand up now and then and "eat a toast" to somebody's success?
>
> —Jerome K. Jerome

REFLECTION

For the victim of booze, there is always lurking fear of solid food: there might be nourishment in it, as well as the prospect of healthy thinking and living, all of which must be avoided.

AFFIRMATION

I'll feast on life itself today, between bites of food taken, with due moderation.

JANUARY 3

Priest to drunk parishioner:
"Don't you know drink is your enemy?"

*"I know, Father, but you told me
to love mine enemy."*

REFLECTION

The devil can quote scripture and mine enemy is just as cunning.

AFFIRMATION

That I may keep from entering into any dialogue with my enemy today—lest the truth be obscured.

January 4

> Faces along the bar cling to their average day:
> The lights must never go out,
> The music must always play.
>
> —W. H. Auden

REFLECTION

Alcohol made our lives very small. It cut us off from those we love and most of all it cut us off from ourselves. We developed a siege mentality. Fear dominated us and the only solace was in the bar and the bottle. We were like children afraid of the dark, convinced we were no good. Sobriety is the beginning of the road back to life when we leave the false security of the bottle and the bar behind us.

AFFIRMATION

Help me to remember that all I have to do is to stay away from one drink one day at a time.

JANUARY 5

He who is master of his thirst is
master of his health.

—French proverb

REFLECTION

The "calms" in our existence are the periods when we maximize joy, love, and creativity. The more of them the better!

AFFIRMATION

O Great Navigator, let me chart my course around the storm, and if I must go through it, let me see just one guiding star.

January 6

The statistics on sanity are that one out of every
four Americans is suffering from some form
of mental illness. Think of your three best friends.
If they're okay, then it's you.

—Rita Mae Brown

REFLECTION

Well, if it's me, then I have a chance, as I found out soon enough to do something about it. There is hardly a soul among us who has not thought he/she was totally cuckoo at one time or another. I know that all my friends have gone bonkers at times, but I'll not mention it if they don't mention MY derailment.

AFFIRMATION

Let me only go inside my own head for housecleaning this day.

January 7

The greatest wealth is to live content with little,
for there is never want when the mind is satisfied.

—George Bernard Shaw

REFLECTION

If I can get out of bed in the morning without groaning and moaning about my hangover headache, and if I can remember where I was last night, and to whom I spoke, and what I said, then the mind is free to outline a good day for me.

AFFIRMATION

Today, all I need will be provided, and whatever I want will be taken into consideration.

January 8

If you drink to forget, please pay in advance.

—Tavern sign

REFLECTION

If we drink to forget a problem, when we regain our senses, we will have several other problems to deal with, i.e. physical debility, financial debility, spiritual debility, and any and all other debilities.

AFFIRMATION

Today, let me put problems in perspective, so that I may deal with them as if they can be resolved without war, bloodshed, or lingering anger.

JANUARY 9

> If you don't clean your house for two months,
> it doesn't get any dirtier.
>
> —Quentin Crisp

REFLECTION

In the life of an active drunk, nothing gets any dirtier. Nothing changes, really, except that the bottle keeps emptying itself and somehow it must be refilled or replaced. We don't notice the accumulation of dirty clothing, dirty dishes, and the stink from our unwashed bodies. After two months . . . or four (if we live), we are oblivious to the wreckage piling up around us.

AFFIRMATION

What I'd like today, O Thou who art next to cleanliness, is a bit of dignity and a laugh to go with it.

January 10

There is in all men a demand for the superlative, so much so, that the poor devil who has no other way of reaching it attains it by getting drunk.

—Oliver Wendell Holmes

REFLECTION

Ah, the dreaming! The grandeur of the mind! The grandiosity of our imaginations and the stupidity of thinking we can elevate ourselves by getting drunk!

AFFIRMATION

This is one day I can elevate myself to great heights by simply getting on my knees and saying "HELP!"

January 11

The graveyards are full of indispensable people.

—Charles De Gaulle

REFLECTION

What if I went off on a super-binge this day? There is a pretty good chance of not returning to normal life due to death or disability. Would I be missed? Yes, for a few months by some, a few minutes by others, but life would go on regardless.

AFFIRMATION

For this day on Earth, let me increase its store of goodness, not deplete it.

January 12

> If life was fair, Elvis would be alive
> and the impersonators would be dead.
>
> —Johnny Carson

REFLECTION

That's the way it is. You can do everything right and all with the best of intentions—and still wind up behind the eight ball. And then suffer the irony of having some guru from the program ask what step you are working on. So much is out of our hands. Learning to accept life as it breaks over us is the hardest of tasks. We are all part of God's plan. The choice is to accept it or wallow in the self-imposed pain of victimhood.

AFFIRMATION

Help me to see beyond the appearance of things and to know that I am always part of God's plan.

JANUARY 13

The saints are the sinners who keep on going.

—Robert Louis Stevenson

REFLECTION

Thank God there are no perfect people; if you found one you would run like hell. We are so wonderfully human, susceptible to good and bad but always trying to somehow do the right thing in the face of so many "easy ways out." So we keep going on, and in the end, the good outweighs the bad and God never stops loving us.

AFFIRMATION

I know there is an inherent decency in all of us. Help me to reach for it when I need to find it.

January 14

> We are never as happy
> or as unhappy as we imagine.
>
> —La Rochefoucauld

REFLECTION

We are all subject to the vicissitudes of life, no matter how sane or together we appear to be. There are days when despite great health and abundance we are tormented and wonder about the meaning of it all; or having achieved great success we feel the emptiness of simply being on the planet. Guess what—it's human. We run from the guy who is always up and run from the guy who is always in the dumps. That's the way it is. Guess we fit somewhere in the middle. It's human.

AFFIRMATION

Help me to accept my place on the planet, and when happiness or adversity arrives help me to accept them both, knowing they too will pass.

January 15

To live in the present is to live in eternity.

—Wittgenstein

REFLECTION

Someone has said that even God can't operate in the future. We honestly don't know if is true or not, but it is certain that projecting into the future removes us from the reality of the present. Living as fully as we can in the day every day is the key to happiness. If we are projecting our lives into some future time when we have all our ducks lined up in a row, we deprive ourselves of whatever joys come to us in the moment and make our happiness contingent on so many things we cannot control.

AFFIRMATION

I know that learning to live in the now is the key to emotional maturity. Projecting into the future is an exercise in futility.

January 16

A politician, on his attitude toward whiskey:

"If you mean the demon that poisons the mind,
pollutes the body, desecrates family life,
and inflames sinners, then I'm against it.
But if you mean the elixir of Christmas cheer,
the shield against winter chill,
the taxable potion that fills public coffers
that comfort crippled children, then I'm for it.
I will not compromise."

—Anonymous

REFLECTION

The dictionary describes "alcohol" as a "colorless, pungent, volatile liquid," and it describes "nicotine" as "a poisonous alkaloid." Both are related in a roundabout way and may be taken in legally, without a prescription. Of course, politicians will take a position on these substances, and they will hide behind the pretense of being against sin and for virtue. Addiction knows no morality; it is an amoral force, entirely unto itself. In old Western movies, they knew well what they were talking about: "What's your poison?"

AFFIRMATION

Today, I'll keep in mind what's my poison and leave it well alone.

January 17

We lived for days on nothing but food and water.

—W. C. Fields

REFLECTION

Many of us discover an astonishing fact of life when we get into recovery. It's hard for us to imagine a morning without the ritual vomiting and the revulsion at the sight of a poached egg. Looking around us, we see millions of normal people, getting through a day joyfully, sans alcohol.

AFFIRMATION

I'll settle for food and water this day—and anything else that's normal.

January 18

> You cannot teach a man anything.
> You can only help him to find it within himself.
>
> —Galileo

REFLECTION

Ultimately each of us has to find our own truth within ourselves. Growing is a process that can only take place in our own hearts and minds. Yes—there is guidance and help but no can do it for us, because that is the way God planned it. Imagine a world in which we all saw things the same way. Just think of how much you would miss the self-righteous arguments and the thrill of trying to convince others just how right and smart you are.

AFFIRMATION

Help me to find my own truth. I pray that I may not hide from it. Help me to grow and to take my place in your divine plan.

January 19

> The most useful and least expensive household repair tool is the telephone.
>
> —Wes Smith

REFLECTION

Isolation is an important component of alcoholism. This disease is like a mad, jealous lover who wants me all to itself. It follows me, interrupts me, and stalks me, and does not want me talking to those who would want to help me. It implores me to remain incommunicado: "Don't answer the phone; don't speak to anyone; don't reach out—they will stop you from drinking, and I, who love you and understand you, will not take away your drink." That's disease jargon.

AFFIRMATION

Let me thank my disease for sharing, and then let me show it to the door as I answer my phone.

January 20

When you are not fishing, be mending the nets.

—Irish proverb

REFLECTION

Whether we are drunk or sober, the world goes about its business. So, 'tis well for us to fit sobriety into a very visible slot so that we can get on with the process of living, working, laughing, and thanking.

AFFIRMATION

My resolve today is to chase away the gloom, even if I have to fake it 'til I make it.

JANUARY 21

Gratitude is the most exquisite form of courtesy.

—Jacques Maritain

REFLECTION

If we take inventory of ourselves, it's likely we will make a list of our defects, and of what's missing, omitted, or destroyed. A healthy person will look at what she has in stock: life, breath, family, health, teeth, limbs, and the possibility of a good day and the chance to make amends to those who were injured in some way. That's gratitude.

AFFIRMATION

Am I ever blessed this day! Let me seize it!

January 22

> When a fool is told a proverb,
> it has to be explained to him.
>
> —Ashanti proverb

REFLECTION

Is the alcoholic a fool? If a man finds out he has cancer and does not seek treatment, he is considered a fool. But if we find out we are alcoholic and continue the old habits, not only are we fools, but suicidal and possibly homicidal as well. It's a deadly prospect.

AFFIRMATION

What kind of fool am I? None, I hope, this day.

January 23

All truth passes through three stages.
First, it is ridiculed. Second, it is violently opposed.
Third, it is accepted as being self-evident.

—Arthur Schopenhauer

REFLECTION

It's almost a cliché that the first casualty in wartime is the truth. Our presidents will lie to us under the pretext of "national security," or from the conviction that we are too fearful or weak to handle the truth. How, then, can we believe a liar when he tells us the truth? I don't, and neither do I have to be his judge. All I have to do is clean up my side of the street.

AFFIRMATION

Am I living a truthful day, without gloating at my own goodness?

January 24

In days of old, the horseman came galloping into the castle courtyard, leapt off the steed, dashed up the stairs, and threw himself at the king's feet:

"Sire, I did as you commanded.
My army has pillaged and terrorized the North."

"Fool!" snapped the king.
"I told you to pillage and terrorize the West!
I have no enemies in the North!"

"You do now, Sire," said the horseman.

—Anonymous

REFLECTION

One of the problems of recovering from alcoholism is finding out the extent of the damage we have done to family and friends in the North or the West, and what to do about making amends. Though that may take time, and forgiveness is uncertain, I'm bound to try for it.

AFFIRMATION

Let not my shame keep me from making amends so that I will do no further harm.

January 25

An Irishman can be worried by the thought that there is nothing to worry about.

—Austin O'Malley

REFLECTION

And you don't have to be Irish to suffer such conflicted emotions. There is another saying: "Don't borrow trouble." Some of us dislike borrowing, so when we seek out trouble, we fully intend to keep it.

AFFIRMATION

If I can go about my life today, I know I have a sackful of solutions. Then, it's unlikely troubles will overwhelm me.

January 26

> We ought to be able to learn some things second hand. There is not enough time to make all the mistakes ourselves.
>
> —Harriet Hall

REFLECTION

Of course, I am not a perfect fool or a complete ass! No human being is a perfect or complete anything, so when I do look at the faults of others, it ought to be with compassion and the hope that I'll not inherit them.

AFFIRMATION

It's a good day to take my personal inventory and a spiritual stock taking to see what I need.

January 27

> The weak can never forgive. Forgiveness is
> the attribute of the strong.
>
> —Mahatma Gandhi

REFLECTION

We, the diseased ones, are usually afflicted with self-righteousness and tales of wrongs done to us. Rotten parents, cruel teachers, brutal police, bad prison conditions, stupid judges, unsympathetic spouses, faithless lovers, angry children. Can we ever forgive them, or, indeed, is there anything to forgive? Who did it to us?

AFFIRMATION

Let me break the cycle of blame by forgiving those I've hurt and wronged for the foolish reason that they haven't forgiven me.

January 28

> Anybody can become angry,
> but do we become angry with the right person
> to the right degree, at the right time,
> for the right purpose, and in the right way?
> That is not within everybody's power,
> and it is not easy.
>
> —Aristotle

REFLECTION

Did I ever think that righteous anger could be such hard and tedious work? It would take me weeks to get all the elements in place, and by then, the object of my anger would have gone elsewhere. Seems to me, anger is a waste of time, energy, intelligence, and spirituality.

AFFIRMATION

Today is the best day to drop my burden. It's too heavy to carry.

JANUARY 29

> I know that what is moral feels good
> and what is immoral feels bad.
> It ain't that complicated.
>
> —Hemingway

REFLECTION

The heart always knows the truth no matter how we may try to hide from ourselves. We all have that tendency to hide a bad motive under a good one, but there is no getting away from the built-in compass of right and wrong. And it doesn't take a college education to figure it out. Being honest with ourselves is a daily workout. You can never let up.

AFFIRMATION

Help me to acknowledge my God-given ability to distinguish between right and wrong, and to take responsibility for all of my actions.

January 30

> If pain could have cured us
> we would long ago have been saved.
>
> —George Bernard Shaw

REFLECTION

There is a myth which says that if we endure enough pain then at a certain point we are assured a wonderful life. It ain't so. Unfortunately some of us become addicted to pain and accept it as our natural state. Yes, life presents us with painful situations, and yes, there is a lot of what seems to be unjust pain. But it is not necessary to volunteer for it or to ask for more than your share.

AFFIRMATION

I know that life will bring painful situations for me; give me the wisdom to move past them to know happiness again.

JANUARY 31

Though I speak with the tongues of man and of angels, and have not charity, I am as a sounding brass or a tinkling cymbal. And though I have the gift of prophecy and understand all mysteries and all knowledge, and though I have all faith so that I could remove mountains and have not charity, I am nothing.

—St. Paul's Epistle to the Corinthians

REFLECTION

Perhaps this is the most telling and profound message of all. It is about giving of oneself—not just money, not advice, not even prayers. It is about putting yourself in the place of the afflicted, the poor, the downtrodden, the dregs who are so despised and mocked because they don't seem to be able to help themselves. The rest is all talk and we all know that in our hearts. How often we resist the natural impulse of the heart to reach out because we are afraid or we are ashamed that they touch us as they do. Follow your heart—the God-given impulse to reach out.

AFFIRMATION

Help me not to be blinded by smugness or to judge those who need help. Help me to understand that in giving it is I who am being given the gift.

February 1

When it is dark enough you can see the stars.

—Ralph Waldo Emerson

REFLECTION

Often, it is when we reach the very depths of our pain and despair that we begin to see the first small glimmer of hope. But why does it have to be that way? Probably because that's what it takes for us to be able to see. At that point we have a choice: either we can go out with a whimper or we can get up and move toward the light. In reality it is the only real choice we have; the stars are always there whether we choose to see them or not.

AFFIRMATION

Help me to see the stars even when they are covered by the dark clouds. Help me to know that you are always there, dear God, even when I am so full of fear and feel so disconnected.

February 2

> We are all mystically united: a mystic bond
> of brotherhood makes all men one.
>
> —Carlyle

REFLECTION

This is another way of saying that no man is an island—yes, we are all individuals, but at the same time we are all connected by and to the Creator. There is something of each of us in all of us. We see ourselves in each other sometimes better than any mirror we look into. When we hear each share at meetings we make that mystical connection. We experience the comfort of knowing that no matter how isolated we may feel at times, the mystical bond is always there waiting for us to connect to it again.

AFFIRMATION

Help me to know that I am never alone. Help me to reach out to others like me and to share myself so that I may find myself.

February 3

> Even God cannot change the past.
>
> —Agathon

REFLECTION

We are stuck with the past, but the Greeks said we could change it by how we choose to see it and by our attitude toward it. But it is good to remember that there are many things of the past we have no need to change. It is all the memory of our ever-evolving selves, and no matter how it may appear, every moment of the past is sacred.

AFFIRMATION

I know there is a pattern that runs through my life from the beginning. Help me to see it and to accept it even when I don't understand it.

February 4

A man should never be ashamed to admit he has been in the wrong, which is but saying, in other words, that he is wiser today than he was yesterday.

—Alexander Pope

REFLECTION

My disease would love to have me declare that I am cured of an incurable condition. Then it could get to work on killing me, as my pride wouldn't say I was wrong.

AFFIRMATION

There is no right way to do wrong, and it's wrong-headed to keep denying my disease. Today, let it all hang out and let the sunshine in.

February 5

> One of the saddest things is that the only thing
> a man can do for eight hours is work.
> He can't eat for eight hours,
> nor drink for eight hours,
> nor make love for eight hours.
>
> —William Faulkner

REFLECTION

Is that a fact? Well, Mr. Faulkner, either you are not an alcoholic or don't know any, but there are some who drink for not only eight but sixteen and even twenty-four hours, and if there is a sniff or two of cocaine available, the drinker's self-destructive horizons are boundless.

AFFIRMATION

O Great Timekeeper, let me take the next hour, enjoying the wonder of life sans alcohol. Now I can breathe, see, feel, hear, taste, and smell all that liberates my life.

February 6

> You can't find God—
> you have to let God find you.
>
> —Thomas Merton

REFLECTION

We were never very good at showing up and we really never wanted anyone to find us, let alone God. The question we heard most was "Where the heck were you?" and most of the time we didn't know the answer. In sobriety we begin to understand the need to act as though we have faith. To know that in truth He has already found us.

AFFIRMATION

Help me to live as though I have faith. I pray to be open to the gift of grace when it comes to me.

February 7

> The first glass makes a man animated,
> his vivacity great, his color heightened.
> In this condition, he is like a peacock.
> When the fumes of liquor rise to his brain,
> he leaps and gambols as an ape.
> Drunkenness takes possession of him,
> and he is like an angry lion. When it's at its height,
> he is like a swine: he falls and grovels on the ground,
> and then falls into a drunken slumber.
>
> —Mohammedan proverb

REFLECTION

Do I need another day like that in my life? Isn't it a blessing that I awake at all, with the freedom to breathe and make a decision about my day and its doings?

AFFIRMATION

Of course, pigs don't descend to drunkenness, so for today, let me be as sober and noble as a pig.

February 8

Speak when you are angry—and you will make the best speech you'll ever regret.

—Laurence J. Peter

REFLECTION

So many of us are gifted with eloquence when drunk or high. It's rare that we recite words of love in that condition; instead we rant and rave at all the dastardly acts that are visited on us by hordes of seen and unseen enemies. We rehearse our brilliant repartee, leaving our opponents speechless and defeated.

AFFIRMATION

I will keep a civil tongue in my mouth, and when I speak, people will be glad to hear me.

February 9

A Cocktail (definition, from the 19th century):

"A stimulating liquor which renders the heart stout and bold and at the same time fuddles the head. Said to be of great use to Republicans, because a person having swallowed a glass of it is ready to swallow anything else."

REFLECTION

Nothing is more repellent to the average healthy person than to be told to take something "because it is good for you"—usually some foul-tasting, unattractive commodity.

AFFIRMATION

Today, I'll be happy to abstain from that which kills me, and maybe tomorrow I'll take that which is good.

February 10

The devil will come to you when you are happy.

—Andre Gide

REFLECTION

The truth is that it takes courage to be happy, and when it is achieved, our demons try to bring us back to our misery. Negativity can be just as addictive as alcohol, and just as destructive.

AFFIRMATION

I pray to be open to all of the possibilities in my life and to receive the gifts of God with an open heart.

February 11

> How can anyone ever know what a man
> has to overcome in himself?
>
> —Oscar Wilde

REFLECTION

Being with ourselves is the hardest thing of all. And as was heard said at a meeting—"Sometimes I'm the kind of guy I would avoid at all costs." Part of the pain of recovery is in risking being alone with all of our unnamed fears and our feelings of inadequacy. Recovery is about letting ourselves receive the help we need to come to our true nature by recognizing our demons and learning to live with them. But we can't do it alone. Share your feelings at meetings and with those close to you. Discovering how similar we are to others helps to relieve our guilt and our isolation.

AFFIRMATION

When I'm enmeshed in the loneliness and isolation of my fear, help me to live in the reality of my recovery and see through the falseness of my fears.

February 12

> There is no meaning to life
> except the meaning man gives his life
> by the unfolding of his powers.
>
> —Erich Fromm

REFLECTION

It is always a difficult proposition to accept—the idea that each of us is responsible for our own lives. I mean we didn't ask to be here, did we? It was Eve who got us thrown out of the garden of Eden. And now I am responsible? It is the same idea as sobriety. Alcoholism is a disease none of us asked for, yet in order to stay sober and grow and mature in life we have to take responsibility for our actions. It is up to each of us to discover and nurture our own powers and to put them to the best possible use.

AFFIRMATION

I pray, dear God, that I may become the person you intended me to be. Help me to find meaning in my life by following your will for me.

February 13

A kleptomaniac called his psychiatrist at 2:00 A.M., yelling that he had an overwhelming desire to steal something. The doctor said, "Take two ashtrays and call me in the morning."

REFLECTION

Some recovering alcoholics will call their sponsor (the person who is the fellow sufferer) to get the bid of counsel when the temptation arises, and, of course, the response will be "Give me one reason as to why you should drink!"

AFFIRMATION

I can think of a thousand reasons to drink, but there is only one why I shouldn't. Let me heed the one.

February 14

> Don't threaten me with love, baby.
> Let's just go walking in the rain.
>
> —Billie Holiday

REFLECTION

For some of us the hardest thing is to accept love when it comes to us. So many of us feel unworthy or believe that those who would give it to us must be lacking themselves. As Groucho said: "I wouldn't belong to a club that would have me." Some of us feel trapped by it or feel that it will overwhelm us. Love must always begin with ourselves. Then we can love and we can be loved.

AFFIRMATION

I pray that I may learn to love myself so that I can love and be loved.

February 15

When Toomey put a frog on the bar and sat staring at it, the barman asked what was going on. Toomey said,

"As long as I can see one frog, I'm sober, but when I see two, I have to take action."

"What action would that be, then?"

"I grab the both of them and put them in my pocket and go home."

REFLECTION

The alcoholic mind is a mad mind, with nothing beyond the bounds of possibility. It's all "real" and all mad. The good news is—unlike other forms of madness, when you stop drinking, the symptoms vanish.

AFFIRMATION

If I stay sober today, my reality will bring me peace.

February 16

> You can't hold a man down
> without staying down with him.
>
> —Booker T. Washington

REFLECTION

For a variety of reasons, some of us think we belong in the gutter: sense of inferiority, race, gender, shame, etc., but we won't go directly, so we'll ride down on an alcohol flume, hoping that no one will notice our descent. It always helps if we can push someone down ahead of us.

AFFIRMATION

I hope to get back my wings today, wash 'em off and fly.

February 17

> If I stop drinking, people will think
> I have a drinking problem.
>
> —Malachy McCourt

REFLECTION

There I go again: "What will people think?" Well, contrary to certain internal alcoholic assertions, I am not the moving center of the universe. A swollen ego only keeps me isolated, where I'm no help to myself or anyone else.

AFFIRMATION

Today, O Controller of Egos, let me just get on with my life and not worry about outside opinions.

February 18

On not drinking, mine!—I say:

"If there are those who mind, they do not matter, and, of course, those who matter do not mind."

REFLECTION

There's an odd anomaly in that many of us who have behaved like colossal assholes in the past under the influence of the grog or drugs now feel we have to apologize for not drinking anymore.

AFFIRMATION

O Lord, today just let me smile and say "Thank You" for all that is good which is offered to me. Life and plain soda are an inebriating combo.

February 19

> I'm Commander, see . . .
> I do not need to explain why I say things.
> That's the interesting thing about being President.
> I don't feel like I owe anybody an explanation.
>
> —George W. Bush (to Woodward)

REFLECTION

Drunks who become dry drunks are vengeful and angry at having to give up the cocaine and the alcohol and will take out their frustration on everyone around them. Dr. Lawrence Green of Texas sez: "If people make behavioral changes without changing their internal values, beliefs, and attitudes, the new behaviors are less likely to stick."

AFFIRMATION

May I be willing to see new, enduring spiritual values, and may the self-righteous mantle disappear from my life and from that of my Leader.

February 20

Liquor is a giant killer, and nobody who has not had to deal with the Giant many many times has any right to speak out against the Giant Killer.

—Ernest Hemingway

REFLECTION

Many of us are still childish when we proclaim, "I can do it myself." Hemingway thought he could, but the Giant Killer got him. Alcohol has a mighty army assembled to kill those of us who have the disease. It has the law on its side, it has society, it has the medical profession that says it's "O.K." in moderation, it has the church, it has history and tradition on its side.

AFFIRMATION

Let me not get into battle today. I'm no coward if I walk away knowing it takes two to stage a war.

February 21

> I have learned silence from the talkative,
> toleration from the intolerant,
> and kindness from the unkind.
>
> —Kahlil Gibran

REFLECTION

In other words, I have to keep learning, no matter what the source. I need only remember my own babble when in my cups, and my fierce, judgmental attitude when others behave as I do and, of course, the damage I have wrought in the past.

AFFIRMATION

It's a good day to remember my character defects and to begin a remedial life.

February 22

An alcoholic is someone you don't like
who drinks more than you do.

—W. C. Fields

REFLECTION

I couldn't possibly be an alcoholic like *that* asshole. We have nothing in common, not even the same brand of whiskey. Moreover, I work hard . . .

AFFIRMATION

O Lord, let me sweep my own side of the street, and let me keep it clean.

February 23

Winning is a habit; unfortunately, so is losing.

—Vince Lombardi

REFLECTION

Winning over the curse of addiction or, as some say, the blessing, is very simple. You begin by not picking up a drink or a drug. By not doing something, we are doing something amazing—we are starting our recovery. That's winning. Choose a bad action, like picking up a drink, and you have lost at least one round.

AFFIRMATION

I'll not bend the elbow this day; maybe I'll bend someone's ear.

February 24

> Better sleep with a sober cannibal
> than a drunken Christian.
>
> —Herman Melville

REFLECTION

This advice takes a bit of cogitating, as the average alcoholic is too socially conscious to be caught snoozing with a cannibal. Good Heavens! What would the neighbors think?

AFFIRMATION

When I drink, it matters ill to me who is in the bed, so today and tonight let me be in command of my senses, so that I'll sleep in peace, safe from rampaging Christians and vegetarian cannibals.

February 25

> The three faults of drink are: a sorrowful morning, a dirty coat, and an empty pocket.
>
> —Irish proverb

REFLECTION

Most people of average intelligence are aware that losing one's senses to drink or drugs can and does have painful consequences, so they stop. The alcoholic knows full well the losses to be endured, and yet will or cannot stop. We have amnesia brought on by a siren's song . . .

AFFIRMATION

As I awaken to a new day, may I be able to say "Thank you for a good yesterday."

February 26

Cornelius returned to the village after years abroad.

Priest: "I hope you were loyal to your faith whilst you were away."

"Indeed I was, Father," replied Cornelius. "I drank, I lied, I drank, I fought, I drank, I blasphemed, I drank, I stole, I drank, I had bad women, I drank, but never, never, never, did I forget my religion."

REFLECTION

We have the tendency to compare ourselves to others and point out what others do that we don't. Cornelius might have comforted himself by saying he never fucked a sheep.

AFFIRMATION

I've made a fool of myself at times; let me not make it my lifestyle.

February 27

Alcohol is necessary for a man, so that now and then
he can have a good opinion of himself,
undisturbed by the facts.

—Finley Peter Dunne

REFLECTION

At no time is an active alcoholic disturbed by facts of any kind. We may get a temporary lift in our opinion of ourselves, but the subsequent drop is very steep.

AFFIRMATION

O, Spiritual Chemist, just give me your nonlethal spirit formula for this day.

February 28

Our deepest fear is not that we are inadequate
but that we are powerful beyond measure.

—Nelson Mandela

REFLECTION

Why is it that we are afraid of our own power? Our own potential? What is it in us that makes many of us hide our light under a bushel? What are those potentialities for knowing and experiencing which we cannot or will not exercise? We were born to make manifest the glory of God that is within us. Our task in life is to free ourselves from the bondage of our self-centered fear and bring our gifts to the world.

AFFIRMATION

I know my fear is nearly always a bogeyman and not based in reality. I want to see my fear for what it truly is. My own dark projection of myself.

February 29

> So, take your share, man, of dope and drink.
> Aren't you the Chairman of Ego, Inc.?
>
> —W. H. Auden

REFLECTION

Indeed I aren't, when nobody's looking. At those times I'm on my hands and knees with a magnifying glass, looking for my ego. Ego is never my friend, so I mustn't feed or embolden it.

AFFIRMATION

O Lord of Feeling, let me not be addicted to extremes. Let me recognize that "normal" is sufficient for today, and until the next Leap Year.

March 1

> If we are peaceful, and if we are happy,
> we can blossom like a flower,
> and everyone in our family
> and our entire society
> will benefit from our peace.
>
> —Thich Nhat Hanh

REFLECTION

I am sober reading this, and I know I cannot change the past, but at this moment I can begin to make amends to those I love and who love me, or even hate me for the horrors I visited on them. I may not be forgiven, but for today I'll not repeat the rotten behavior of the past.

AFFIRMATION

Let me today keep my mouth shut about my formation. Today I will do what is good without ostentation or fanfare.

March 2

> Faith consists in believing when it is
> beyond the power of reason to believe.
> It is not enough that a thing be possible
> for it to be believed.
>
> —Voltaire

REFLECTION

That idea puts paid the theory of "the hopeless case." The two accursed words to be avoided in our language are: "I can't"; wait, add two more: "Not possible." There is no human being (who's not dead) beyond recovery and redemption.

AFFIRMATION

My goals today: 1. Stop that which is killing me; 2. Begin that which gives me life.

March 3

> I have a small flickering light to guide me
> into the forest. Up pops a theologian
> and blows it out.
>
> —Mark Twain

REFLECTION

Truth cannot be imposed upon us from without. The spiritual journey is about finding your own truth and religion or dogma cannot do it for you. They may help but they can't replace your own conscious contact with God. There is no mass salvation, each of us has to follow our own hearts, and we sometimes have to tell the theologians to get lost.

AFFIRMATION

Help me to believe in my own truth and my own vision. My relationship with the Creator is mine and nothing can take it away from me.

March 4

There exists an obvious fact that seems utterly moral:
namely, that a man is always a prey to his truths.
Once he has admitted them,
he cannot free himself from them.

—Camus

REFLECTION

There is no more uncomfortable creature than a person with a bellyful of booze and a head full of A.A. suggestions. Schizophrenia barely describes the condition.

AFFIRMATION

My sanity is in mine and God's hands today; let me be aware.

March 5

When the 'arf made recruit goes out to the east,
'E acts like a babe and drinks like a beast,
And he wonders because he is frequently deceased.
'Ere he is fit to serve as a soldier.

—Rudyard Kipling

REFLECTION

As is often said, the alcoholic is indeed King Baby, who wonders all the time why he is not being fed and pampered by adults, and why it is he dies at all because of a few drinks.

AFFIRMATION

If I don't live sober, I will die drunk, and never see the face of my Maker.

March 6

If drinking too hard makes a drunkard,
wouldn't thinking too hard make a thunkard?

REFLECTION

There is indeed what is known as "stinking thinking," and 'tis that leads us to the hospital or the jail. The person who recognizes stinking thinking is on the way to recovery.

AFFIRMATION

Let me strip the shiny wrappings from my treasured thoughts so that I may walk a sober path.

March 7

Don't look for answers. Love the questions
and perhaps you'll live your way into the answers.

—Rilke

REFLECTION

There are many questions for which there are neither answers nor explanations. So much of what comes to us in this life is inexplicable. Life happens and we can't play God and demand answers. When we live through the situations life brings us we get the chance to begin to understand how necessary they were to our spiritual journey.

AFFIRMATION

I accept life as it comes to me, confidant that what I need to know and understand will be revealed to me by living one day at a time.

March 8

> When men began to drink,
> they burst into song like birds.
>
> When they drank more,
> they became strong as lions.
>
> When they drank too much,
> they became stupid as asses.
>
> —Swiss mural

REFLECTION

I would be delighted to sing like a bird and to have the courage of the lion, and Man is more stupid than any ass if he fails to know he becomes impaired after too much drink and still continues. (Asses don't drink alcohol because they are either too stupid or too smart!)

AFFIRMATION

O Lord, if stupidity will keep me sober, let me be stupid this day.

March 9

> "My country right or wrong"
> is something no true patriot
> would ever think of saying.
>
> It's like saying,
> "my mother, drunk or sober."

REFLECTION

A drunken mother is like any other drunk: someone flattened by alcohol. Being a mother or a patriot does not lessen the power of the disease, though some folk will think it's a sign of devoted motherhood or patriotism to get drunk on certain occasions.

AFFIRMATION

As a parent today, let me show by example that sobriety is the best path, and may my mouth open only to smile at my family.

March 10

> No man thoroughly understands a truth
> until he has contended against it.
>
> —Ralph Waldo Emerson

REFLECTION

When the truth is simply that we are murdering ourselves with alcohol, the first thing, of course, is to deny it. Therein is the first contention. When the landscape becomes littered with the wreckage of my life, it might occur to me that I should accept the truth and begin a process of recovery.

AFFIRMATION

If there is anything amiss in my life, may I accept the truth of it and take action.

March 11

> I inherited a vile melancholy from my father,
> which has made me mad all my life,
> or at least, not sober.
>
> —Samuel Johnson

REFLECTION

The good doctor complained of what was done to him in life. He wrote profusely on all that bothered him, and, unlike the rest of us, he got paid for his bitching and moaning. If there is no benefit in complaining about heredity, 'twould be as well to find out what I liked about my father.

AFFIRMATION

If my addiction is handed down, let me drop it in the nearest grave so that I may live and not pass it any further.

March 12

> When you cease to make a contribution
> then you begin to die.
>
> —Eleanor Roosevelt

REFLECTION

Every one of us is vital to the Creator and all that we have to give is what is expected of us. If we ever reach that point where we feel that we no longer have anything to give, we must turn our thoughts around and affirm again that, as God's children, we are needed for the full duration of our presence here. Chances are that you have far more to give than you realize.

AFFIRMATION

I need to remind myself of all that I have to give. I will always seek opportunities to be of use to others and to myself.

March 13

No one person on this planet can make you happy. It already has to be in you.

—Vernon Duffy

REFLECTION

If only we could find the one person who would make us happy forever. Then we wouldn't have to do anything else but search. But we know in our hearts that unless we have the capacity for happiness in us, it is not going to come from some other person, place, or thing. Amazing just how often we are told that most things in life begin and end with us. Wish there was some secret formula or a hidden tome that would reveal something different. But it just ain't so.

AFFIRMATION

I understand that I am responsible for my own happiness. It begins and ends with me.

March 14

> Learning is suddenly understanding something you've understood all your life but in a new way.
>
> —Doris Lessing

REFLECTION

It is amazing how we think we know something only to rediscover it and see it for the first time again. Experience deepens our knowledge and our vision. We cannot cling to the same world view all of our lives. Life unfolds in ways we never expected, and we find that many times we are forced to see things we thought we were sure of in a whole new light. It is what they call wisdom.

AFFIRMATION

Help me, dear God, to always be open to new understanding and to be willing to change as circumstances and clearer vision dictate.

March 15

> Come away, O human child!
> To the waters and the wild
> With a faery, hand in hand,
> For the world's more full of weeping
> than you can understand.
>
> —"The Stolen Child,"
> by W. B. Yeats

REFLECTION

Too many drunks and druggies have dispatched themselves and their children from this earth, be it by automobile, by house fire, or by violence. Dry drunks inflamed by power have dispatched hundreds of thousands of young people to die for love of country, when in reality it's lunatic power and madness disguised as patriotism for which it's being done.

AFFIRMATION

Lord of place, protect me from anger and violence this day, so that I may not harm any human being. May there be peace in my day.

March 16

> A saloon is madness sold by the bottle.
>
> —Jonathan Swift

REFLECTION

We alcoholics think we are getting a bargain when liquor prices drop, when in fact we are merely paying less for more insanity.

AFFIRMATION

Today, let me be aware of the high price of insanity, no matter if it be for free.

March 17

> When God made time, He made plenty of it,
> so what are you rushing for?
>
> —Irish proverb

REFLECTION

There is no need to rush headlong into sobriety so long as I do not drink anything in the way of booze today, or ingest anything else in the drug department. If I abstain today, I can begin a nice, slow recovery, and time will not be the only factor.

AFFIRMATION

O True Friend of the Drinker, help me assuage all thirsts and cravings by the simple act of drinking a pure glassful of water.

March 18

> Too often opportunity knocks,
> but by the time you push back the chain,
> push back the bolt, unhook the two locks,
> and shut off the burglar alarm, it's too late.
>
> —Rita Coolidge

REFLECTION

There is always the guy who will tell you he never got a break in his life and behind him there is a trail of lost opportunity. Sometimes we are so afraid of failure that we set up impenetrable walls of resistance. The world comes looking for us and we have put out a Do Not Disturb sign. Stop hiding. The world is out there waiting for you. Just show up and there will always be another opportunity.

AFFIRMATION

Help me to unlock the door to my life. I pray for the courage to follow the light to happiness and fulfillment.

March 19

> What is man but a minutely set, ingenious machine for turning red wine into urine?
>
> —Isak Dinesen

REFLECTION

If it were as simple as that, the body besotted with wine would merely be a cleansing machine. But my body is in constant search of perfection and will assume that what I put into it is for that purpose and will send the wine careening into all my organs. Alcoholic bodies cannot deal with wine; they process it 'til it is a poison.

AFFIRMATION

Let me give the body only what it needs this day. Alcohol is the last thing the temple needs!

March 20

> People drink for hereditary reasons, social reasons,
> because they are tired, bored or restless.
> People drink for as many reasons as they have
> for wanting to feel better.
>
> —Alfred Kazin

REFLECTION

Some of us drink because we have a disguised disease that loves us on the surface and is plotting our murder under the surface. And so it is that drinkers will find any excuse to get high, if they're so inclined. The "reasons" may be bogus or genuine, but they all land you in the same ditch. Happiness is never the outcome.

AFFIRMATION

Remind me, Divine Pal, that there are innumerable reasons to drink, and only one to stay sober: my life.

March 21

Change is certain—progress is not.

—E. H. Carr

REFLECTION

Progress does not come automatically. Unfortunately, it requires a willingness to constantly look at ourselves and then be willing to accept what we find and act upon it. It is not easy. And sometimes our best efforts seem to leave us where we are. Change comes far easier than progress. And sometimes we only realize we have advanced long after it has occurred. The key is to stay willing even when we know we don't have the answers. Keep on truckin'.

AFFIRMATION

We seek progress not perfection and it will only come in God's time not mine.

March 22

> The essence of being human is
> that one does not seek perfection. . . . Just progress.
>
> —George Orwell

REFLECTION

It is sheer folly to try to be perfect. Even if you did achieve it, who the heck would want to be around you? And then you probably wouldn't be able to tolerate all of us imperfects around you. So relax and rejoice in your humanity—that wonderfully imperfect state you were born into.

AFFIRMATION

I rejoice in my imperfection even as I strive for growth and progress.

March 23

> The highest possible stage of moral culture
> is when we recognize the need
> to control our thoughts.
>
> —Charles Darwin

REFLECTION

We all know the expression "Garbage in, garbage out." Perhaps the most lethal of all of man's afflictions is negativity, and it begins inside each of us. There is a dark side to us where the real battle of life and death takes place. That is the reality of existence. Know your enemy. Become familiar with him. Know how he operates. He is you.

AFFIRMATION

Help me, dear God, to be ever aware of my own propensity for negativity. Help me to understand my own basic mistrust of life and the world. Help me to believe in the great gift you have given me.

MARCH 24

> "I think I have seen you somewhere,"
> said one man to another.
>
> "No doubt," said the other.
> "I've been there often."

REFLECTION

Somewhere, anywhere, nowhere . . . How the hell do we know where? It's over the rainbow for some of us, and with blackouts we know not where at any time. Again, "drunk time" is lost time, and I can't afford such losses.

AFFIRMATION

I need to be aware of my whereabouts on any given day, particularly this one. Isn't this where I'm supposed to be?

March 25

They don't sell tickets to the past.

—Alexander Solzhenitsyn

REFLECTION

The problem is that we don't have to buy tickets to get there. It's a free show, so many of us spend far too much time in that region. The old axiom is: Look back but don't stare. We can't have the regrets or the bad breaks of the past dictating our attitudes today. Take the good and don't dwell on the pain and the hurts. The possibilities of today far outweigh the pain of the past.

AFFIRMATION

I pray that I may not let the past steal the possibilities of the future. Help to stay in the now and believe in God's plan for me.

March 26

> Preacher: "Put a worm in water and it thrives.
> Put a worm in whiskey and it dies."
>
> Lesson for the alcoholic:
> "If he keeps drinking whiskey,
> he will never get worms."

REFLECTION

We alcoholics are wonderful at rationalization, and we are walking encyclopedias of the "benefits" of drinking alcohol, most of which are nonexistent.

AFFIRMATION

May I remember that some people die from eating peanuts, and that may be my fate, allergic to alcohol as I am, if I drink today.

March 27

> A blow with a word strikes deeper
> than a blow with a sword.
>
> —Robert Burton

REFLECTION

Sarcasm and putdowns are the prerogatives of the coward, afraid of self-examination, lest he be found wanting. No one wants or needs to be judged by his inferiors.

AFFIRMATION

May all my words today be in praise of that which is good in myself, the human family, the earth . . .

March 28

> I am larger—better than I thought.
> I did not know I held such goodness.
>
> —Walt Whitman

REFLECTION

We have somewhere come to believe that we have to be very hard on ourselves, like harsh parents. It is so hard for many of us to acknowledge our talents and our own good nature. So hard to see the goodness in ourselves as others see it. Take a good look inside and you will be surprised to see that your own judgment is flawed. You are better than you think and have a great capacity for goodness. It is your responsibility to see that.

AFFIRMATION

Help me to understand that I am inherently good. Help me to dispel the idea that I am bad and undeserving.

March 29

Nobody holds a good opinion of a man
who has a low opinion of himself.

—Anthony Trollope

REFLECTION

If you don't believe in yourself then who will? Absorbing this is often very difficult for many of us. We feel like phonies even as family, friends, and co-workers recognize our achievements and our abilities. Our doubt can lead to self-destructive actions. At the back of it is a kind of pride that rejects the powers which God has given us. We must look at our talents with gratitude and understand that they were given to us for the fulfillment of God's plan for us and his creation.

AFFIRMATION

I must take responsibility for the gifts that God has given me. God believes in me. I must know and accept that fact.

March 30

> Dragons breathing fire are just silly mythical beings getting rid of resentments.
>
> —Malachy McCourt

REFLECTION

There is hardly a being alive who hasn't made a full course banquet of some resentment—thundering herds of thought shutting out all civilized discourse and sentiment, with our consent, driving us to insanity. We never forget to breathe the good air in the midst of the reenactment of our hurt. Dragons do it better: they blow it all out!

AFFIRMATION

Remind me to breathe deeply today, and to douse all inner fires of my smoldering anger.

March 31

The demon of intemperance ever seems
to have delighted in sucking the blood of genius
and generosity.

—Abraham Lincoln

REFLECTION

Lincoln was a man who understood the disease of alcoholism. He had compassion for those who suffered from it, though the thinking of the time held that temperance was a reflection of willpower and good character.

AFFIRMATION

Even though it is a disease, I have the personal responsibility this day to do all I can for my recovery. Let me not bullshit myself that I am helpless or powerless.

April 1

Coincidence is God's way of remaining anonymous.

—Bill Moyers

REFLECTION

It is amazing how the most amazing things happen to us when we least expect them. The confluence of events, situations, and personal actions often contrive to produce results we could never have imagined. And it seems somehow that there was some unseen influence operating, doing things we couldn't do ourselves. Coincidences happen too many times to too many people to be random acts. There is a lot to be said for the idea of breaking God's anonymity when we know in our hearts who is really in control.

AFFIRMATION

I know that God is working in my life even when my thoughts and actions are removed from any awareness of his presence. Help me to remember that He is always with me.

April 2

> God created alcohol to keep the Irish
> from ruling the world.
>
> —Jonathan Swift

REFLECTION

God created fire, too, for human benefit, but in the hands of an arsonist, it's a deadly force. Likewise, a soothing draft of alcohol becomes a toxin in the hands of an alcoholic.

AFFIRMATION

All I need to rule today is my desire to drink. May I be near water all day.

April 3

> One reason I don't drink is I want to know
> when I'm having a good time.
>
> —Nancy Astor

REFLECTION

When the booze hits the gullet and societal curbs abscond, I am apt to believe I'm enjoying myself. I then confuse not being unhappy with happiness, and in the morning I'm still confused, in addition to having a sore head.

AFFIRMATION

O Lord, let the good times roll, but not over me.

April 4

An alcoholic atheist is a man
who wishes to God he could believe.

—A paraphrase of Dr. John McLaffy

REFLECTION

As the condition is one of "lacks" (lack of physical health, lack of emotional stability, and lack of spirituality), the victim knows he is in desperate need to get surcease from the pain. So, of course, we say contradictory things and angry things against God, who doesn't arrive unless invited.

AFFIRMATION

This day, I'll take into my life a God Who doesn't mind if I perspire and Who likes laughter.

April 5

> The man who starts out going nowhere
> usually gets there.
>
> —Dale Carnegie

REFLECTION

It's an old illusion we get from alcohol—that we are in the midst of creative life. Great thoughts flow, magnificent speeches come to mind, and witty retorts. Sophistication reigns, and then we fade into a blackout, awakening to a miserable headache, and an empty pocket—once again . . . nowhere.

AFFIRMATION

I'll set a goal for today, and it will include staying sober.

April 6

Reality is that which, when you stop believing in it, doesn't go away.

—Phillip K. Dick

REFLECTION

Some very clever people have said, "What's so great about reality?" There may well be nothing perceivably great about it, but reality is oddly inevitable. We can experience part of it if we drink *real* alcohol, get *real* drunk, and learn that the bars in prison cells are *real* steel. We may also find out that sickness is really sickening, and loss is very real.

AFFIRMATION

Today, I'll take great joy in the realities of being.

April 7

> A hangover can be defined as
> "when the brew of the night
> meets the dawn of the day."

REFLECTION

Hangover: "to loom over; left over from another state or condition."

Another's miserable condition tends to bring a smile to the healthy one's lips. Hangovers are a combination of bodily toxicity and spiritual poisoning brought on by drinking. The cry goes up, "'Twasn't me; it was the booze that done it!"

AFFIRMATION

If I hadn'ta done it, it wouldn't ha' done me. Divine Spirit, save me from the night before before the night before.

April 8

Imagination is more important than knowledge.

—Albert Einstein

REFLECTION

Imagination is at the beginning of all creativity. It lies at the heart of every possibility. It is the divine idea made into reality and its potential is infinite. It is as necessary to us as arms and legs. Without it we could never rise above ourselves or our condition. It is God's way of expressing himself through us.

AFFIRMATION

Help me to nurture and acknowledge my own imagination. It is God's way of talking to me.

April 9

> Bob was caught in a snowstorm,
> so he sent a message to his office
> saying that he wouldn't be in today
> as he hadn't arrived home from yesterday yet.
>
> —Anonymous

REFLECTION

One of the results of dropping in at the local watering holes is that that's where we halt all progress in our lives. The illusion of "active life" pervades the joints, but like those models who are the picture of health in cigarette ads, their glamorousness misleads us: it is a coffin with silver handles.

AFFIRMATION

All long journeys begin with one step; the road to recovery is the same. Let me take it today.

April 10

> You cannot be angry at people
> when you laugh at them.
> Humor teaches tolerance.
>
> —W. Somerset Maugham

REFLECTION

It is a good idea to always try to see the humor in a situation. Sometimes it just isn't there and we just have to look past it. As has been said: "Dying is easy—comedy is hard." Sometimes it's a matter of laughing at ourselves. When we can laugh rather than get angry or blame another, we have a victory. And the greatest victories are always those we win over ourselves. Of course, if you laugh too much the men in the white coats might take you away, but still the victory is yours. Ha, ha, ha.

AFFIRMATION

I know that laughter is a great tranquilizer. I pray for good humor and the ability to see myself in the folly of others.

April 11

> The young disease that most subdue at length,
> Grows with his growth and strengthens
> with his strength.
>
> —Alexander Pope,
> *Essay on Man*

REFLECTION

Alcoholism is like being invaded by parasites and cancer. We don't know when we have been invaded, but very subtly the disease becomes us and takes over all our human functions. In ancient Irish mythology, people thus altered were called "changelings."

AFFIRMATION

If I'm willing to listen, I can be a co-physician with a Higher Power to expel all invaders from my body this day.

April 12

> If at any one moment in time there was
> more evil being done in the world than good
> it would all go up in flames.
>
> —Carl Jung

REFLECTION

There is an irresistible tendency to believe in the negative. To see the world as going to hell in a handbasket. It may well be as someone said: God didn't create this place in one week but put it all together on one very bad day. The reality is that bad news always will travel faster and be remembered longer than the countless acts of good and the billions of kindnesses that happen every minute of every day. We are as inherently prone to good as we are to evil, and believe it or not, the good seems to be winning.

AFFIRMATION

God, help me to see beyond the appearance of things. Help me to know that beyond all evidence to the contrary, the world is a mostly wonderful place.

April 13

> When a reformed drunkard gives advice,
> you don't hear it, you see it.
>
> —Dr. Seldon Bacon

REFLECTION

'Tis often said that whosoever can take advice is sometimes better than the giver. And 'tis often said, "Take my advice; I'm not using it myself." If my mind is clear and free of drink, however, I can recognize good advice, no matter the source, since "good advice is sometimes given by bad people."

AFFIRMATION

Today, let my life's doing be the best advice of the day, and may I hear it myself.

April 14

> On a rough sea voyage, Kevin groaned
> that the only thing keeping him alive
> was the hope of dying.
>
> —Irish Bull (Anon.)

REFLECTION

Some of us can't go on sea journeys, even on canoe trips, without suffering seasickness. Yet, we keep on tripping in the hope of one day finding our sea legs. So it is with the addict: we hope to ingest or imbibe with no ill effects.

AFFIRMATION

If needs be, let me stroll on a canal tow path, surrounded by the serenity of nature and the song of birds.

April 15

> Pride, envy, avarice: these are the sparks
> Have set on fire the hearts of men.
>
> —Dante,
> *Inferno*, Canto II

REFLECTION

The fire that seeks to be quenched by alcohol of course only fuels the flames. Who among us has not been hit by false pride, bitter envy, and smoldering avarice? O poor, poor me, left behind as the world goes on its merry way.

AFFIRMATION

It is a splendid idea to take a positive inventory of what I have on this day: breath, feelings, senses, and life itself will do for now.

April 16

Never let the future disturb you.
You will meet it, if you have to,
with the same weapons of reason
which today arm you against the present.

—Marcus Aurelius,
Meditations, 200 A.D.

REFLECTION

We need never worry about the future, as it is bearing down on us at all times, and no matter how we twist and turn, we can never move out of its path. Some folks go to fortune tellers, but never to "misfortune tellers." They want to hear about wealth, health, happiness, opportunity, and general good fortune. It's well that the future comes to us in small chunks, the size of a day.

AFFIRMATION

Whatever is in the cards or the crystal ball, bring it on! I can and will deal with it!

April 17

> It is hard to fight an enemy
> who has outposts in your head.
>
> —Sally Kempton

REFLECTION

Our enemy in sobriety is negativity, which is the most active limb of the disease of alcoholism. It will set up an encampment on any terrain, and train its guns on our most vulnerable areas. Oddly enough, the best way to defeat it is by not fighting it. Simply say, "Thank you for your visit; now pack up and leave the grounds, as I've got a lot of growing to do."

AFFIRMATION

If I keep the doors of my mind open today, they will not be battered down.

April 18

Man is not born wicked;
he becomes so as he becomes sick.

—Voltaire

REFLECTION

If we can go through this life exploring and investigating that which enhances health and well-being and avoiding that which sickens us, then we have a good chance of a full life.

AFFIRMATION

O Lord of Explorers, let me look at the menu of life and give me the wisdom to order only what is good and needed.

April 19

> Reality is an illusion
> created by the lack of alcohol.

REFLECTION

Another kneeslapper for us saloon denizens: Alcoholics, addicts, and gamblers seek happiness through murder of the senses. Thus, we cannot ever be of service to our fellow humans.

AFFIRMATION

Let me know reality, O Lord, that I may do some good whilst here on this earth.

April 20

The alcoholic eventually takes the form
of a whiskey bottle—
all neck and belly, and no trace of a head.

—Austin O'Malley

REFLECTION

The spectacle of the headless chicken comes to mind. Are we any less absurd or close to death, floundering, thrashing, all the while imagining that we're in control of our lives?

AFFIRMATION

If I can keep my wits around others who are losing theirs, I may be tempted to use them. Tempt me, O Lord!

April 21

> A lifetime of happiness? No man could bear it.
> It would be hell on earth.
>
> —George Bernard Shaw

REFLECTION

Life seems to be made up of achieving the right combination of opposites. Even the very best foods require seasonings that are themselves unpalatable, but used in correct proportion produce the meals of gourmets. Opposing forces operate within each of us. Learning to balance them creates the platform upon which we may be open to true happiness when it comes. For many it is an acquired taste, something to appreciate and savor, knowing that it will not last forever.

AFFIRMATION

I know how important balance is in my life and I will try to always work for the kind of equilibrium that allows me to function best.

April 22

> Anxiety occurs at the point where
> some emerging potential or possibility
> faces the individual which at the same time
> involves eliminating his present security.
>
> —Rollo May

REFLECTION

We dread change even when it means it will lead us to a happier and more fulfilling life. Why is this? There is the idea that the devil you know is easier to deal with than the one you don't. It seems to be part of human longing that we will find one situation, one place, where we can go easily through our lives with the minimum amount of distress. This amounts to having a pipe dream. Life is about change and if we avoid bringing our attributes to fruition because of fear, then we can only know anxiety and a loss of our true nature.

AFFIRMATION

God, help me to overcome my fear of the world. Help me to trust in the potential you have given me. Help me to understand that it is only by fulfilling your will for me that I can find serenity.

April 23

> We have to know that we can never
> be separated from God. Each of us is a part
> of his mystery and even our despair
> and our misery cannot remove us from him.
>
> —Thomas Merton

REFLECTION

God does not move in and out of our lives. He is ever-present in all of us. Whether we are conscious of his presence or not is up to us. We have to know that we are like a ship moving through a fog, and the horizon and the stars are still there even though they can't be seen. God is ever-present and will always hear our appeals for help and guidance.

AFFIRMATION

Dear God, help me to be always aware of your presence in my life. Help me not close myself from that presence by disappointment, or the conditions that prevail. Help me to understand that despite appearances you are always there for me.

April 24

> We are all in the gutter but some of us
> are looking at the stars.
>
> —Oscar Wilde

REFLECTION

It is all about attitude. And that is perhaps the one thing in our lives we can control. It has to do with vision: the belief that although we may be in difficult or even really painful circumstances today, it will not stay that way forever. Those who survived the concentration camps during World War II were those who, despite their daily hell, maintained a vision of the future. It is the hardest concept of all to practice because sometimes all we have going for us is our faith. Even in the darkest night of the soul the stars are shining behind the clouds.

AFFIRMATION

Help me believe that You are always at my side, dear God. Help me to see through the darkness to the light of your love.

April 25

> I was much further out than you thought
> and I wasn't waving I was drowning.
>
> —Stevie Smith

REFLECTION

We are all adept at appearing to be "fine," to our friends and even to our families. It has been said that we alcoholics are the greatest actors in the world. We have played every role in the book and some that have yet to be written. Showing our vulnerability and our need for the love and help of others is hard. Many wait until it is too late to ask. Comedy is tragedy from a distance AND IT AIN'T FUNNY. Always wave before you are too far out.

AFFIRMATION

Help me to reach out for help before I let circumstances overwhelm me. Help me to overcome my ego and belief in my own tragedy.

April 26

Men must live and create—
live to the point of tears.

—Camus

REFLECTION

It is not enough just to make our way through life without making a contribution. The idea is to leave something positive behind because that is why we are here. You are God's own special gift. Your presence is necessary to God's plan. And sometimes this proposition is hard to take. Sometimes we are like Sisyphus pushing the rock up the hill, only to see it reach the top and roll back down again. Even in our tears and disappointments we have to understand that we are made the way we are to do what God has assigned us to do.

AFFIRMATION

Help me to put what I have into the world, dear God. Help me to hold nothing back and help me to understand that even in the midst of pain and disappointment you are with me.

April 27

> A gamekeeper saw a beautiful naked young woman walking toward him in the woods.
>
> "Are you game?" he asked.
>
> "I am," she said.
>
> So he shot her.

REFLECTION

Some people think the world is divided between the hunters and the hunted. This is cynical, perhaps, but partially true. We don't have to be naked game or hunted, but we can fall into either role by our way of living.

AFFIRMATION

When I take a walk in the woods, let it be a meditation in motion, untainted by fear.

April 28

> Gratitude is at the beginning
> of all positive change.
>
> —Leonard Holzer

REFLECTION

Gratitude is the surest way to induce a sense of grace into our lives. It is so easy to let our needs and wants and disappointments conceal the positives. Unhappiness usually starts with a sense of being a victim because our lives aren't exactly the way we would like them to be. The truth is they may well never be the way we want them, so we have to acknowledge those parts of our lives that work well and be grateful for them. If we want positive change then we must begin by being grateful for where we are.

AFFIRMATION

I will never measure my life by the standards of the world. I pray to accept my life as it is and to move forward in gratitude for all of the possibilities it may show me.

April 29

> An honest man can feel no pleasure
> in the exercise of power over his fellow citizens.
>
> —Thomas Jefferson

REFLECTION

Being honest is not merely saying things. Some of us think we are being truthful when we point out defects in other people's characters. Of course, we are just being self-righteous and judgmental at such times. True honesty is difficult, since it is almost beyond the capacity of ordinary humans. All we can do is be thoughtful and considerate of ourselves and others in all of our doings.

AFFIRMATION

Today, I'll not confuse being right with being honest.

April 30

> I didn't hurt or kill anyone today,
> and I didn't take a drug or a drink,
> and I prayed for a few bastards I couldn't stand,
> so it was a good day.
>
> —Michael Glynn

REFLECTION

There's a man not overly exercised by ambition for the day, or unduly disturbed by hate or disturbed by certain people. He went about his life with good cheer, and went to bed reasonably happy.

AFFIRMATION

Let me steer the ship of mind into calm waters.

May 1

> Drinking first takes the drunkard out of society,
> and then out of the world.
>
> —Ralph Waldo Emerson

REFLECTION

There were no automobiles in Emerson's day, but still the drinker died prematurely. The causes were as varied as they are today, but they were sometimes disguised by the medical profession and shamed families as "natural" deaths. In truth, they were brought low by failed livers, by freezing, by falls from horses, by accidents with tools, murder, and, most dreadful of all, by suicides.

AFFIRMATION

There is a time to die, but let it be in Nature's plan for me, and let it not be today.

May 2

We alcoholics drink on two occasions:
when we are thirsty and when we are not.

Repeat, we alcoholics drink on two occasions:
when we are alone and when we are with others.

REFLECTION

The occasion for drinking is simply being alive and in the presence of alcohol. The need for sober action is on any occasion, such as when we are breathing.

AFFIRMATION

Just for now, let my inhalations be the free air of the earth. Eating, drinking, and all others can wait until I've savored the joys of sobriety.

May 3

Note to Boss:

"Dear Sir: I'm sorry my husband, John,
can't come to work this week,
as he is suffering awful pain brought on
by acute indiscretion."

REFLECTION

There goes the old disease again, involving the family in its dirty doing. It makes fools of all of us one way or another, even to writing blooper letters that send workplaces into fits of cruel laughter.

AFFIRMATION

If I'm not able to get to a place today, I'll be responsible for informing those who need to know.

May 4

Where Satan can't go in person, he sends alcohol.

—Jewish proverb

REFLECTION

Whether or not we believe in Satan, who is the personification of what is known as "the devil," and a host of other names, the fact is that the disease of alcoholism is personal, friendly, powerful, baffling, cunning, and it is evil. Evil, because its mission is to destroy our lives. "Live" spelled backwards is "evil," and it's backwards it wants us to go.

AFFIRMATION

Today, let me keep moving forward one step at a time with a song in my heart.

May 5

> The thing I fear the most is fear.
>
> —Montaigne

REFLECTION

The prospect of being afraid terrifies us. It is never so much what is going to happen that we're afraid of as it is the reality of being in the grip of fear. And most of our fears are rarely rational and nearly all of what we fear never happens. When we feel vulnerable and helpless it is hard to find that sliver of reality to hang on to. We lose ourselves and we act out, often with disastrous results. There is a guy who was a white-knuckle flier for years. He really believed that it was his fear that kept the plane in the air. One day he realized that 747s were built to fly. He was relieved but he was disappointed that his fear had no bearing on how he got to San Francisco.

AFFIRMATION

God, please find me when I am in the grip of fear. Help me not to lose sight of your presence in my life. Help me to know that there is always a way through it with your help.

MAY 6

Maturity is the capacity to withstand
the ego-destroying experience and not lose
one's perspective in the ego-building experience.

—Robert K. Greenleaf

REFLECTION

We have to learn to treat those two imposters success and failure the same. Maturity is about achieving balance in our lives—this means emotional balance. Bill Wilson wrote that few would achieve this but nevertheless the journey is about accepting our being as we are and growing at the same time.

AFFIRMATION

God, please help me to understand that being able to accept the ups and downs of life as they come will bring me closer to you. Help me to always know that you are always at the center of my being.

May 7

Self-deception is the surest way to self-destruction. Reality has a way of catching up with us.

—Sam Erwin

REFLECTION

There is the guy who goes to AA for a few weeks and then goes back out and begins to drink again under an assumed name. The only guy he's fooling is himself. Sobriety cannot come to any of us without self-honesty.

AFFIRMATION

Help me to always be able to see through my own spin on myself. I know that reality checks are essential using the fellowship.

May 8

The veteran army sergeant wasn't feeling well one night and went to the doctor.

"When did you have a drink last?" the doctor asked.

"1955," the sergeant replied.

"That's a long time without a drink," sez the doctor.

"Sure is," sez the sergeant.
"It's nearly 2130 right now."

REFLECTION

Time is of no importance or consequence to the mind when it's in the grip of the disease. One day morphs into another, and hours are only important as they concern the opening and closing hours of liquor stores and saloons.

AFFIRMATION

If on the twenty-four-hour clock I am able to check off the sober hours, I'm winning today.

May 9

> You can do very little with faith
> but you can do nothing without it.
>
> —Samuel Butler

REFLECTION

As the saying goes, faith will move mountains; but the real question is who the heck would want to move them? For most people faith has more to do with how we act than how we think: How we go about doing what we have to do when it all seems so meaningless. It is the unseen hand that moves us to do what we have to do even when we are caught up in our negativity.

AFFIRMATION

I pray that I can always listen for the still small voice which whispers to me from within, and that God will always find me when I can't find him.

May 10

Alkies go berserk at ship's launchings due to what's
being done to perfectly good champagne.
At one reported launching, 'twas said:

"The Duchess smashed the bottle of champagne
against the ship's bow amidst applause
as she slid on her greasy bottom into the sea."

REFLECTION

I need to remember the slides into the slime and muck in the shameful past, and that 'twould be better if alcohol bottles were spilled outside of me rather than wasted within me.

AFFIRMATION

May my thirst be slaked by love today.

May 11

> We are healed of suffering only
> by suffering it to the full.
>
> —Marcel Proust

REFLECTION

Nobody in their right mind would recommend suffering if it could possibly be avoided. None of us want to be martyrs, although I'm sure we all know a few who would leap at the chance. The thing is that whether we want it or not, suffering is going to come to us. And in most cases there is no way around it. Let it wash over you. Trying to avoid it is more likely to kill you than accepting it and taking your lumps. And it is indeed true that you will have really made a great gain at the end of it.

AFFIRMATION

When suffering comes, I pray that I may have the courage to accept it and go through it as best I can.

May 12

The trouble with Ashcroft is that
when he is not drunk he is sober.

—Yeats

REFLECTION

The trouble with that comment is implying that being sober is the opposite of being drunk. Being drunk means temporary deprivation of the goodness we inherently possess. Sobriety means spiritual health, serenity, decency, openness of heart, generosity, and love. All else is just being "dry."

AFFIRMATION

O Friend of the Deprived, grant me the grace to seek sobriety, and to be able to see when I'm merely "dry."

May 13

> Alcoholism is not a spectator sport;
> eventually, the whole family gets to play.
>
> —Joyce Burditt

REFLECTION

Many of us proclaim that, even if we are alcoholics, we are hurting no one but ourselves. That's another alcoholic delusion, as we do not behave like human beings to our families or to our communities, and we become a burden to society when we get to the looney extreme.

AFFIRMATION

Let me be a loving, supportive member of my family and a joyful, active member of my community this day.

May 14

> Some mornings it doesn't seem worth it
> to gnaw through the leather straps.
>
> —Eno Phillips

REFLECTION

Not all of us end up in the cuckoo department, having been handed over by the blue coats to the white coats. However, the chances are reasonable that we will find ourselves wearing a restrictive garment if we keep drinking. Due to neglect, our teeth will not do the gnawing job, so we might as well resign ourselves to D.T.s, or recover.

AFFIRMATION

Just for today, I'd like to use my teeth to eat the food of my choosing.

May 15

> A man's true wealth
> is the good he does in the world.

REFLECTION

Alcoholics will rationalize that because we spend a lot of money on wine, beer, whiskey, gin, and vodka, we are keeping the economy strong, which is like saying that because we urinate and defecate, we keep the sewage industry strong. There are enough people who drink moderately so that I need not worry unduly about the booze economy.

AFFIRMATION

There is no excuse for drinking when I am an alcoholic—not today, not any way.

May 16

> It ain't what a man don't know
> what makes him a fool
> but what he does know that ain't so.
>
> —Josh Billings

REFLECTION

If I don't take a drink today, if I give thanks for one more day of life, if I can enjoy the rain, accept the snow, not worry about the sleet, take a stroll in the sun, say a kind and encouraging word to a crying child, hug a grieving friend, there's not much else I need to know today, except to eat well.

AFFIRMATION

What do I know today? I know enough to smile at what I know.

May 17

> To love oneself is the beginning
> of a lifetime romance.
>
> —Oscar Wilde

REFLECTION

To love oneself is to accept the gift of life that God has given us. And yet so many of us can only see some Dracula staring back at us in the mirror each morning. Where do these terrible feelings of unworthiness come from? What is it in us that drives a wedge between ourselves and the Creator? Some mornings Dracula is gone and we are looking at Rodney Dangerfield. A famous abbot said that we were not created but loved into existence. If God is Love, then we are His Love personified. The only task we have is to truly love ourselves as God loves us. You will be surprised to see yourself one morning and that face will be smiling back at you.

AFFIRMATION

I want to love myself truly. It is the only way for God's grace to enter my heart.

May 18

Chase after truth like hell and you'll free yourself, even though you never touch its coat-tails.

—Clarence Darrow

REFLECTION

Chasing after the truth is great exercise, and it's a great goal for us. Unlike the mechanical hare at the greyhound track, there is always a possibility of catching up with the truth. Sometimes, it's there for the taking, even if we don't always avail ourselves of it.

AFFIRMATION

My mantra this day: "The truth shall set me free to deal with deception."

May 19

> Remember that fear always lurks
> behind perfectionism. Confronting your fears
> and allowing yourself the right to be human can,
> paradoxically, make you a far happier
> and more productive person.
>
> —Dr. David M. Burns

REFLECTION

Many of us know that "FEAR" is an awkward acronym for "Fake Expectations Appear Real." I don't have to confront my fear; all I have to do is say, "Hello, Fear. It's time for you to move on."

AFFIRMATION

May all my fears be known to me this day and not lurking as in a nightmare.

May 20

No man who is in fear or sorrow or turmoil is free,
but whoever is rid of sorrows and fears and turmoils,
that man is by the selfsame course
rid also of slavery.

—Epictetus, Book 2

REFLECTION

If I have to fret about when, where, and how I am to get a drink, a drug of any sort, or a cigarette, then I am not free. I'm not free to breathe, to sleep, to walk about, or to travel. The question arises, "Why am I doing this to me, of all people?"

AFFIRMATION

If I don't know I'm enslaved, then I cannot know freedom. O Lord, let me know the truth.

May 21

> Drunkenness is the ruin of reason.
> It is premature old age
> and temporary death.
>
> —St. Basil

REFLECTION

A drunk is as reliable and trustworthy as a jet plane at 35,000 feet with two dead pilots. No one knows when it will plunge to earth, with all the resultant devastation. For the alcoholic, there is no control over drinking, so to begin life, we need to stop drinking.

AFFIRMATION

Let me remember it's the first drink that starts my dying process, and I may not come to life again.

May 22

> They say a reasonable amount of fleas
> is good for a dog—keeps him from brooding
> over being a dog mebbe.
>
> —Edward Noyes Westcott

REFLECTION

Many of us do not accept what we are, be it a man, a woman, older, or younger. Some are thinner, some are fatter, some gender preferences are troublesome, and some of us resent the racial group we are born into. So—what to do?

AFFIRMATION

Well, repeat after me: God grant me the serenity to accept the things I cannot change, etc. . . .

May 23

> Perfect knowledge and appreciation
> beget natural temperance.

REFLECTION

If we had anything perfect as human beings, we'd be close to God; but the only perfect act of mine has been one whole day of twenty-four hours without alcohol, followed by another. I appreciate that perfection.

AFFIRMATION

May the memory of sobriety be as sharp and clear tomorrow as it is today, so that I'll try to do nothing but the right thing all day.

MAY 24

> Sitting in a saloon
> is an exercise in isolation.

REFLECTION

One of the symptoms of the disease is a need to be alone but not lonely. Saloons appear to contain all the ingredients of life: light, color, music, talk, coming and going, good cheer, and abundance of spirits, so one can be in the world but not of it.

AFFIRMATION

There's good company at A.A. Let me seek that this night.

May 25

Alcohol has existed longer than all human memory, and for most it will continue to be a servant of man; but for some of us, it will always be master.

—Morris Chafetz

REFLECTION

Alcohol in a bottle is harmless; in an alcoholic's body, it is deadly. It's a weapon that our disease uses when we are not looking to edge us into the grave.

AFFIRMATION

Today is the day to leave it in the bottle. I'm too thirsty to drink alcohol.

May 26

> We are all in the last analysis, alone.
> And this basic state of solitude is not something
> we have any choice about.
>
> —Anne Morrow Lindbergh

REFLECTION

Perhaps this is the hardest reality to face. But what does it mean? Nobody can live our lives for us and nobody else can take responsibility for us. Even though I am surrounded by family and friends I am still alone. We create many diversions to avoid this reality but at the same time it is comforting to know that it is always between me and God. And that is a relationship each individual has to forge for himself.

AFFIRMATION

I understand that I am alone, dear God, but still I know that you are always with me.

May 27

> In order to excel you must live as though
> you are never going to die.
>
> —Marquis de Vauvenargues

REFLECTION

At first glance it would appear that the idea of living as though we were never going to die is kind of a wild notion, an invitation to indulge the spirit of recklessness or to give an excuse to crazy behavior. Some of us don't need any excuse. And besides, nobody's ever gotten out of here alive anyway. But we are talking about not putting limitations or our abilities and achieving all that we are capable of. We all know that there are limits to how long each of us have, but that fact should not limit our own capacity to live to the fullest extent and always be open to what life has to offer.

AFFIRMATION

I know that we live finite lives. I won't let fear of those limitations limit my capacity to participate in my life to the fullest.

May 28

> If you keep saying things are going to be bad
> you have a very good chance
> of becoming a prophet.
>
> —Isaac Bashevis Singer

REFLECTION

Negative projection is a habit and is probably just as addictive as smoking. Just as we use the ritual of lighting up to "soothe" ourselves, we use negativity to insure that when the bad comes we can say with great authority, "I told you so." We use our negativity to separate ourselves from the wonderful possibilities that life has to offer us and that we have to offer life. It is a way of saying no and of insuring our success as prophets.

AFFIRMATION

Help me to break the habit of negativity, to understand that this mistaken idea of self-protection shuts out God's grace.

May 29

> To dispute with a drunkard
> is to debate with an empty house.
>
> —Publius Syrus

REFLECTION

There's no doubt about it: when I'm drunk, I'm talking to myself—not to the person listening—and it's a debate I'll lose. When I do that, there is only self-righteousness and finger-pointing at other folks' deficiencies.

AFFIRMATION

Today, let me accept that all I need to do is take a character defect of mine own and see if I can dismantle it.

May 30

Guide, to bus full of tourists in Dublin:

"We are now passing the Guinness Brewery."

"You might be," sez the alcoholic tourist, "but I'm not. I hear they give free beer to tourists."

REFLECTION

Thought: the alcoholic mind is a bad skier, so 'tis best to stay off any slippery slope. Anyhow, the joke is always on the drinker.

AFFIRMATION

May I remember I have no need to explore the source of my addiction; it's enough that I have it.

May 31

> Breathing out, I know I am breathing in;
> Breathing in, I know I am breathing out.
>
> —Meditation of Thich Nhat Hanh

REFLECTION

The addict alcoholic is like every other human being in that he (she) has a marked tendency not to breathe deeply or appreciatively of Nature's fresh air. Nor do we notice flowers blooming, the sound of a tree sighing in the wind, an eagle soaring, a sunset, a full moon, and a sky full of twinkling stars.

AFFIRMATION

O lord of Nature, if I am to be intoxicated, let it be by the gifts of the senses. No cost, no hangover, and no remorse.

JUNE 1

> Life itself is revolutionary,
> because it constantly strives
> to surpass itself.
>
> —Thomas Merton

REFLECTION

Life demands of us that we achieve greater consciousness—which means that we continue to attain an ever-increasing awareness of reality. There is no standing still in life. It is the same principle of either moving away from a drink or moving toward one. Life demands that we continually grow and develop an ever-increasing awareness of the gift of life itself.

AFFIRMATION

Help me to understand that life is an ever-evolving process of growth and awareness. The more I grow the more is demanded of me. Help me to bring the best of myself to my life each day.

June 2

Sign over too many bars:

"Work is the curse of the drinking class."

REFLECTION

Nothing is more self-contradictory than this cliché of the alcoholic. It takes focus, effort, energy, time, money, diligence, and attention to get drunk. Now if that isn't work, what is?

AFFIRMATION

Achieving sobriety begins with *not doing* something, i.e. not taking the drink. After that, it's only a simple but easy task to seek the reward of sobriety. "Go ahead, God, make my day!"

JUNE 3

Whiskey drowns more men than water.

—Irish proverb

REFLECTION

There is among the drinking fraternity a tendency to rationalize. I call us the "I Only" brigade. "I only" drink beer; "I only" drink wine; "I only" drink "name it." A physician tells a drinker, "Your limit is two drinks a day." The drinker calculates one bottle of wine equals one shot of whiskey, ergo two bottles of wine are OK, and what harm if I have two more?

AFFIRMATION

I simply have to remember I "only don't drink alcohol today" to free myself of the need for phony calculations.

June 4

It is easier to be wise for others than for ourselves.

—La Rochefoucauld

REFLECTION

How much easier it is to see what others need to do for themselves. There is a great satisfaction in solving others' problems, and such a tremendous disappointment when we realize that ours are still with us. It is good to be there for others but better to be there for ourselves.

AFFIRMATION

Help me not to be distracted from my shortcomings by involving myself in solving the problems of others.

June 5

The alcoholic went to his new priest
to take the pledge again:

"How long do you wish to abstain from alcohol?"
sez the priest.

Alcoholic (impatiently): "I always take it for life!"

REFLECTION

I need to remember the future is not here, and I have no control over it, and I cannot get drunk on tomorrow's drink, nor sober on yesterday's pledge.

AFFIRMATION

May I remain sober for now, for this day.

June 6

> Joy is only a symptom of attained power.
> It comes not from submission nor abnegation
> but from assertion.
>
> —Nietzsche

REFLECTION

Joy is the honest expression of being at one with God. In that instant when it comes we are as close to Him as we can be. It is an expression of accepting all that He has given me and gratitude for the gift of life itself. God does not say bow down but rather rise up in assertion of the power and strength you have been given.

AFFIRMATION

I pray that I may not be any less than the person the Father intended me to be. Help me to accept joyously what I have been given.

JUNE 7

The world is always ready to receive talent
with open arms.

—Oliver Wendell Holmes

REFLECTION

One of the gifts of sobriety is the freedom to use our talents and gifts to the limit. There is nothing to hold us back but fear, which often expresses itself in procrastination. You were given these gifts because the world needs them. It needs the very best of every man and woman given life on the planet. If you hold back you may be depriving the world from moving forward the way that God wants it to. Go for it!

AFFIRMATION

Help me to bring my talents to the world. Please don't allow me to hide them under a bushel. Thy will, not mine, be done.

June 8

When the alcoholic was recovering from a severe bout of drinking, which lasted a couple of years, he explained the seriousness of it to a friend:

"The first time I got out of bed and looked in the mirror, the only way I recognized myself was by the sound of my voice."

REFLECTION

Whatever did he say when he glimpsed himself in the mirror? If he is a typical alcoholic, he would be forced to deny that he was himself. I suppose an "Oh, My God, who is that apparition?" would throw some light on the spectacle.

AFFIRMATION

I'd not mind seeing myself in a mirror in the morning if I can say, "'Twas a good night and a sober one."

JUNE 9

> How do you make an Irish cocktail?
> Take a half a glass of whiskey
> and add it to another glass of whiskey.
>
> —Anonymous

REFLECTION

The names we have for drinks are so bland and inoffensive! A "martini" sounds nonlethal; how about "mimosa"? Maybe "Harvey Wallbanger" might hint at danger, but it's still fun. "Tom Collins" sounds like an amiable fellow, while "Manhattan" suggests a pleasant jaunt to the Big Apple. And who could seriously fault a "Brandy Alexander"? Doesn't "Irish Coffee" contain the main necessities for life, caffeine, alcohol, dairy, and sugar? A beer or glass of wine or cocktail? What's the objection?

AFFIRMATION

I wouldn't want to take the risk, so I'll leave the drink to those who still drink.

June 10

> Some alcoholics' prayer is
> that the laws of the universe be annulled.
> Such prayer made by a single petitioner
> is confessedly unworthy.
>
> —Ambrose Bierce

REFLECTION

Some of us confuse prayers with wishes. The God of our understanding answers all prayers, and sometimes the answer is "no." To the active alcoholic, it is not unreasonable to wish for an unlimited supply of booze and to be able to drink night and day AND enjoy life AND have good health. What's wrong with this picture?

AFFIRMATION

All I need to know is that today I'll get pretty much what I need.

June 11

> The noblest question in the world is
> "What good may I do in it?"
>
> —Ben Franklin

REFLECTION

It starts in our own hearts, the good does. I can dispose of one situation by resolving that, a day at a time, I will not pick up a drink or a drug. That frees me to go and do something for other human beings, be they spouse, a child, or an older person.

AFFIRMATION

If I decide to stay sober, there's no better day than today, and no better minute than this one.

June 12

> We need never clone one species: the alcoholic. What you would get is the same old, same old.
>
> —Malachy McCourt

REFLECTION

No matter how fast we run, or how swift we swallow the drink, if we have the disease, there is no cure: there is only the miracle of recovery. But there's no outrunning it or giving it to someone else.

AFFIRMATION

Today I can accept that I am me and, if willing, I'm fully able to change.

June 13

> If ever I need silent stupefaction
> in the company of active alcoholics,
> I need only bring up the subject of
> "alcoholism as a disease."

REFLECTION

The cliché, "Denial is not a river in Egypt," bounds around the world, trotted out by fresh-faced converts to sobriety, bringing pained looks to the faces of those who have been through "recovery" thousands of times. Yet, it strikes a chord because no one of us can claim innocence in the matter of denial, and we'd rather not be reminded.

AFFIRMATION

Let me be enthusiastic about all the new-found joys of sobriety.

June 14

> Men occasionally stumble over the truth,
> but most of them pick themselves up and hurry off
> as if nothing ever happened.
>
> —Sir Winston Churchill

REFLECTION

Churchill wouldn't be exactly an apostle of truth, but the truth is he was a clever man. Sometimes, the truth of the "truth" of our situation is not welcome. For example, I find out that my bank account is depleted. Is that a good or bad truth? If I slip into denial and continue writing checks, I'll go to prison, so 'tis best to confront the truth, whether good or bad.

AFFIRMATION

Truth is being responsible, no matter what. I know I'm equipped, so today let me do what's right.

June 15

Change has a considerable psychological impact on the human mind. To the fearful, it is threatening because it means that things may get worse. To the hopeful, it is encouraging because things may get better. To the confident, it is inspiring because the challenge exists to make things better.

—King Whitney, Jr.

REFLECTION

To conservative minds, change means that they are an extinct species. All alcoholics have conservative tendencies, and are fearful of, judgmental about, and terrified of change. The bar has to be open with the same barman, and the brand has to be available, and all people must behave as if I'm not drinking.

AFFIRMATION

Today, I'll welcome the absence of destructive substances in my life. Sobriety alone will change the mood for the better.

June 16

> If we truly wish to learn, we should consider our enemies to be our best teachers.
>
> —Dalai Lama

REFLECTION

It follows, doesn't it, that our enemies, be they liquid, solid, human, or animal, will create extreme difficulties for us, and in overcoming these difficulties, we learn what to do. Ergo, if the enemy wasn't there, we wouldn't have had to learn anything.

AFFIRMATION

In the school of life this day, let me be a very good student.

June 17

No power on Earth has such influence to terrorize and make cowards of men as the liquor power. Satan could not have fallen on a more potent instrument with which to enslave the world. Alcohol is King!

—Eliza Steard

REFLECTION

The prisons are overflowing with people who did the dirty criminal deed whilst drunk. All across the world, there are children beaten and brutalized by drunken parents, who will then follow in their footsteps—if they make it to adulthood.

AFFIRMATION

Let me today make at least one child happy, and may I never again frighten another human being with my drinking.

JUNE 18

> Alcohol is a threat to women because
> it releases men from the moral control they learned
> from ministers and mothers alike.
>
> —Alice Rossi

REFLECTION

We can't always use alcohol as the excuse for attacking women, only as an explanation. But whether excuse or explanation, we must pay the price by accepting responsibility for any and all criminal acts.

AFFIRMATION

Let me be at peace this day, and all my demons be neutered by grace and love.

June 19

> Over the lips, and down to the liver,
> Come on, whisky, make me quiver!
>
> —Redd Foxx

REFLECTION

Here we go with the clever rhyming witticism! The problem with alcoholism is that it is powerful and cunning—enough to outfox the fox, or any Foxx!

AFFIRMATION

Today, I'll stay out of the foxholes and bask in the sunlight of sobriety.

June 20

> Drink all you want, but don't be a drunken shit.
> I drink—get drunk every day—
> but I never bother anyone.
>
> —Ernest Hemingway

REFLECTION

If ever the caveat, "Take my advice, I'm not using it," was applied, 'twas with this extraordinary man. A drunken human being is a bother to everyone, and to get drunk deliberately makes him a shit, especially when he finally blows his brains out.

AFFIRMATION

May I be safe from stupid pronouncements this day, or sane enough to retract if I do make one.

June 21

> Who knows himself a braggart,
> Let him fear this, for it will come to pass,
> That every braggart shall be found an ass.
>
> —Shakespeare

REFLECTION

The active alcoholic is a combination of cold beer and hot air. There is no subject we won't expound on, particularly when we know little or nothing about it.

AFFIRMATION

Just for today, let me shut the mouth, open the ears, and extend the helping hand.

June 22

> A great man is he who does not lose
> his child's heart.
>
> —Mencius

REFLECTION

They say that the great World War II leader Winston Churchill was childlike and exasperated skeptics with his refusal to knuckle under to the overwhelming odds against overcoming Hitler. Many in fact thought he was impractical and merely humored him as a way of controlling him. Keeping our childish hearts is our affirmation of our closeness to God and our belief in ourselves. It is an attitude that allows us to trust that all is possible no matter what difficulties we may face.

AFFIRMATION

Help me to keep my childish heart despite whatever pain or difficulty may lie ahead. Help me to keep my childish heart which looks inward to God.

June 23

A famous British barrister was noted for his love of card games and his scruffy appearance. John Philpot Curran said to him:

"You don't know how puzzled we are to know where you buy all your dirty shirts."

REFLECTION

Not the most negligible aspect of the deteriorating alcoholic is the physical one. We rationalize the few extra days of wearing the same shirt, and no one can see the underwear, and the socks are far from the nostrils. . . . Showers take up precious time.

AFFIRMATION

Cleanliness may be next to godliness, but it's a sure bet that stinkiness will not be next to anyone. I have the time to be clean and tidy.

June 24

> The fearful banality of evil exists in such normal and banal places.
>
> —Hannah Arendt

REFLECTION

Evil more often than not doesn't appear in the guise of devils or demons but is more likely to take on the trappings of the business office or the stultifying drabness of bureaucracy. It finds its place when we stop seeing others as human, and when we can allow ourselves to be deceived by the expedience of the moment and the justification of "the opportunity for advancement." If your heart tells you something is wrong chances are it is. Evil occurs when we stop listening to the still small voice within us and when we turn a blind eye to the truth.

AFFIRMATION

I know that evil is a reality—the dark side of man—and it often manifests itself as goodness and benevolence. I will work to recognize it for what it is.

June 25

Your playing small doesn't serve the world.

—Nelson Mandela

REFLECTION

There are many who tiptoe through life in the hope that they won't be noticed and that not too much will be asked of them. It is called hiding. They take on a false humility, saying "Look at me, I'm nothing." At the back of this is fear and a refusal to believe in what God has given them. We all have a right to be here and God has given each of us what we need. Each of us is unique and absolutely necessary to God's plan for the universe. So come out come out wherever you are. The jig is up.

AFFIRMATION

Help me to understand, dear God, that I am necessary to your plan. Help me to know that if you didn't want me I wouldn't be here. Help me to put forth what you have given me into the world.

June 26

> Lying to ourselves is more deeply ingrained in us than lying to others.
>
> —Dostoyevsky

REFLECTION

Self-deception is as old as mankind. In the face of reality it is not hard to see why. Let's face it—life can be very hard and sometimes lying to ourselves seems the only way to make it palatable. The problem is it always catches up with us. Comes a time when there is no place to hide. Or that we are not who we thought we were. But underneath the deception is the real you, who is just fine and doesn't need that internal spin doctor.

AFFIRMATION

The only thing that is required of me in this life is to be true to myself.

June 27

> Most of our platitudes notwithstanding,
> self-deception remains
> the most difficult deception of all.
>
> —Joan Didion

REFLECTION

It seems that the one person on the planet we are most desirous of deceiving is ourselves. This is because the most difficult thing for us to do is to accept ourselves as we are, flaws and all, to understand once and for all that you may never play centerfield for the Yankees. That's tough but it's true. It's also true that you are terrific just as you are. The antidote to self-deceit is self-acceptance.

AFFIRMATION

God, please help me to accept myself as I am, warts and all, and to fully accept the wonderful attributes that you have given me.

June 28

"BIRTHS, MIRAGES, AND DEATHS"

—Irish newspaper typo

REFLECTION

It starts as good as can be, and then the drinking, the nightmare, the hallucinations, illusions, delusions—snakes, scorpions, rats. Oddly enough, there are never peaceful visions, or bucolic settings, or heavenly music—nothing but fear, terror, and horror. Am I sick to keep drinking, knowing I'll be invaded? Yes, I am.

AFFIRMATION

I'd like to awaken to whatever reality is in my life this day, be it sunny, rainy, or just a day.

June 29

The future will always hold opportunities
as it will also hold pitfalls.
The key to this dilemma is
to seize the opportunities, avoid the pitfalls
and get back home by 6 P.M.

—Woody Allen

REFLECTION

If you make it home by eleven you're still okay. None of us are going to always make the right life decisions. Mistakes and wrong judgments are a guarantee of our imperfection as many of us have a very real propensity for shooting ourselves in the foot. The only requirement is that we do the best we can each day and accept ourselves no matter how it all turns out. Just don't expect to get time off for good behavior.

AFFIRMATION

God, help me not to shoot myself in the foot, to seek help and direction before I make choices, to understand that left to my own devices my chances aren't so good.

June 30

> Making love all year round,
> and drinking when we are not thirsty,
> is all there is to distinguish us from other animals.

REFLECTION

It's a rare animal that sets out to lose its senses or take its own life. A deer, or even a bear, will be eaten by its predator if it's not fully alert. Aside from lemmings, no animal cops out on its responsibility.

AFFIRMATION

There is little I can do about being human except to be as good at it as I can be.

July 1

> Two roads diverged in a wood,
> and I—I took the one less traveled by,
> and that has made all the difference.
>
> —Robert Frost

REFLECTION

Being true to ourselves is never easy. The world calls out for the norms, conformity, and the willingness to adapt ourselves to the system. The thing is, if you can live with that, okay; but if you find yourself stifled and unhappy in your conformity, then you have to risk taking the road less traveled which will lead you to yourself. Your task is not to please the world and those close to you but to be true to your own spirit.

AFFIRMATION

God, give me the courage to be the person you intended me to be.

July 2

> Abuse of drink is from Satan.
> Wine is from God,
> but the drunkard is from the Devil.
>
> —Increase Mather

REFLECTION

It's the Disease, Stupid! Whether it comes from God, Satan, or from Texas, it kills. It's not a matter of character or weakness thereof. It is insidious, devious, and malicious.

AFFIRMATION

Today, let me help another sufferer so that I may better understand myself.

JULY 3

There will never be a system invented
which will do away with the necessity for work.

—Henry Ford

REFLECTION

Work is another four-letter word ending in "K" which does not produce the same reaction as the "F" word. However, righteous people are always babbling that they work hard and pay taxes, never with a smile or a sign of joy. Why should our movements, our creativity, our imaginations be stifled by approaching work as if it were punishment for sin? God Himself insists we earn our daily bread.

AFFIRMATION

Work or play, whatever I'm to do will be done with least resistance.

July 4

> Very often our virtues
> are only our vices in disguise.
>
> —La Rochefoucauld

REFLECTION

It is amazing how easily virtue can be turned into vice. Bill Wilson referred to it as hiding a bad motive under a good one. It can also be called manipulation—verbal body English strong-arming us into thinking we are trying to do something good. In reality we are simply trying to get our way. Or look big and generous when our intentions are selfish and small.

AFFIRMATION

God, please help me to be always aware of my capacity for self-deception. Help me to think clearly and to approach all of my dealings as honestly as I can.

JULY 5

> No one can really understand
> the grief or joy of another.
>
> —Franz Schubert

REFLECTION

The miracle of creation is that no two people are alike—each of us is a unique part of the creation. So no man can truly walk in another's shoes and no matter how deep our level of intimacy we remain individuals. But we don't have to understand each other—all that is required is an ear to listen or a hand to reach out. All of us need to feel accepted and heard and to know in our individuality we are all connected.

AFFIRMATION

I pray that we may all be united in our individuality. Help me to always see myself in others. I don't have to understand, I just have to accept.

July 6

> The man who loves danger
> shall perish in it.
>
> —Irish proverb

REFLECTION

It is not known how many people are killed each year by alcohol. We can tote up the number of deaths due to drunken driving, and the number caused by liver disease, but some others are concealed by families and physicians because of the shame of addiction. Most heavy drinkers have had enough mishaps to know the dangers of overindulgence, so we stop. But danger itself is addictive.

AFFIRMATION

The dual question of the day: What is worth dying for? What is worth living for?

July 7

I drink, therefore I am.

—W. C. Fields

REFLECTION

There's a life built on a liquid foundation. Does the man jest, and should I laugh and join him? Can I not see the warning in his bitter irony?

AFFIRMATION

Let me keep a sense of humor, O Lord, but help me not to be stupid in thought, deed, and particularly, word. Words especially can trip me up at times when I need good judgment.

July 8

A well-known drunk was invited to a fancy dress ball, and was confused as to what he should go as. His wife suggested: "Go sober!"

REFLECTION

There is hardly a one of us alcoholics who is content with what is given us in body, mind, intellect, or class, so we try to enhance or escape, and in the process destroy what is given us.

AFFIRMATION

Let me have a good look at God's handiwork and help me make it look good too.

July 9

Anger makes you smaller, while forgiveness forces you to grow beyond what you were.

—Cherie Carter-Scott,
If Love Is a Game, These Are the Rules

REFLECTION

There is no end to the damage caused by anger. It knows no morality, no sensitivity to suffering. It is a self-manufactured explosive device, which any man, woman, child, or animal is putting into full production. Our prisons are full of people who gave vent to anger, and our hospitals are full of people who were its victims.

AFFIRMATION

Let me take a deep breath, a cold shower, and put on a smile, 'ere I give vent to any anger.

July 10

> An alcoholic is like the javelin thrower
> who won the coin toss and elected to receive.
>
> —Malachy McCourt

REFLECTION

If it can be done wrong, with spite, malice, and without compassion, sensitivity, or decency, then all that needs to be done is to recruit an alcoholic. Now, of course, I don't mean to "do it"—it's just we had a few drinks, and I wasn't thinking.

AFFIRMATION

Let me withdraw from all competitions this day: I've declared a truce. Rivalry only degrades us.

July 11

> I'm a great believer in luck,
> and the harder I work,
> the luckier I get.
>
> —Stephen Leacock

REFLECTION

If we are lucky, we will meet someone who will influence our decision to get a sober life. That's "luck," but it does subsequently take a bit of work to say, on a daily basis, "No thank you" to the seductions of our disease.

AFFIRMATION

So, all I have to do today is say "No thank you" to my nice disease and suggest a warm place for it to go.

July 12

It costs money to die of cirrhosis of the liver.

—P. G. Wodehouse

REFLECTION

From every point of view, cirrhosis is a bad investment. You turn yellow, and then the damn organ explodes and you die.

AFFIRMATION

For today, let me let my liver live in peace. I may be able to leave it to someone.

July 13

> Unlike tennis, where only 50 percent
> of the players lose, it's a 100 percent loss
> in the alcoholic struggle.

REFLECTION

Somehow, we think we are going to beat the odds. In vain, hope springs eternal. We read avidly of systems which will allow us to drink in moderation by changing brands, changing beverages, drinking later in the day, lining the stomach with milk, butter, or grapefruit juice, drinking slowly, and so on. They never work.

AFFIRMATION

The only winners in the alcohol business are those who sell the stuff. I don't need to drink it today.

July 14

> Survival is not the highest value of life
> nor is it the preservation of our potential.
> The most important thing we can do
> is to express that potential.
>
> —Nietzsche

REFLECTION

What is your relationship to your own potential? Many of us have been involved in avoiding this fundamental aspect of ourselves because we fear our own powers. If we truly follow our gut feelings—our own innate truth—then we are afraid the sky will fall on us and we will be exposed. God did not intend for us to hide our gifts under the scratchy blanket of security. It is not about becoming. It is about being right now. You already are.

AFFIRMATION

God, please free me from the bondage of self-centered fear. Help me to be open to all of the possibilities of life, especially to those experiences that will bring me to my own truth and so closer to you.

July 15

Facing your own mortality isn't some kind of theory.
It isn't an exercise you do in your head.
It is a reality that is at the bottom
of everything you do whether you choose
to acknowledge it or not.

—Hemingway

REFLECTION

The truth is that nobody ever got out of here alive, yet many of us continue on as though mortality doesn't exist. Every day is precious yet we can't wait for everything to work out the way we want it in order to be happy. All we have is today and as far as we know they haven't come up with the eternity pill yet.

AFFIRMATION

Dear God, I know I have a limited time here on earth. Help me to do the very best I can each day and to grab at joy and happiness when they come my way.

July 16

> Strong drink is not only the devil's way into man;
> it's man's way to the devil.
>
> —Adam Clarke

REFLECTION

If I have a pain in my chest, I can say 'twill go away, that it's indigestion, or I'm having a heart attack. The sensible among us will seek out the physician to find out what the condition really is. The fearful will deny anything is wrong, as will the denier. The healthy one will immediately seek help in getting well. The bad part of us says, "Don't bother . . ."

AFFIRMATION

Today, let me face the truth so that I may be healed.

July 17

In Fame's temple, there is always a niche
to be found with rich dunces,
importunate scoundrels, or successful butchers
of the human race.

—Anonymous

REFLECTION

Some of us try to escape into isolation and darkness, and others roar out into the world, dominating the landscape so loudly no one will know we are drunks. We are called "colorful" and entertaining, and fame comes on us simply for being well known.

AFFIRMATION

O Lord, I'm an empty vessel today. Fill me up with God gas so that I'll not be a fool one more time.

July 18

> If bullshit were music, the average alcoholic would be a brass band.
>
> —Paddy Crosbie

REFLECTION

Even the most incoherent of us alkies can be quite eloquent on how it is we are not slaves to drink, and anyway, if we are, it's those around us who are driving us to it, and if only they would shut up about it, we might think of stopping, and so on . . .

AFFIRMATION

One thing I need to know today is: Am I an eloquent fool for the defense of drink?

July 19

> Ordinarily he was insane,
> but he had lucid moments
> when he was merely stupid.
>
> —Heinrich Heine

REFLECTION

An alcoholic is ordinarily insane when in the grip of a very sane disease. Stupidity comes into play when he knows he has a lethal condition which he has the power to alter, but doesn't. It's then that stupidity and insanity are woven into a fabric never to be shredded.

AFFIRMATION

Is there anything more I can do this day other than saying "no" to drink? I could also say "Thank you for allowing me to pass you by."

July 20

> It's not that some people have willpower
> and some don't. It's that some people
> are ready to change and others are not.
>
> —James Gordon, M.D.

REFLECTION

There are many kinds of power other than willpower. My willpower got me to the bottom and now maybe I'll try a higher power. That "wind power" can send me soaring higher than my artificial chemical high.

AFFIRMATION

If I can't find a higher power this day, I am willing to be *found* by a higher power.

July 21

> Take three chorus girls, and three men,
> soak in champagne 'til midnight,
> squeeze in an automobile. Add a drunken driver.
> Serve at eighty miles per hour.
> Chaser: A coroner's inquest.
>
> —1920s Recipe

REFLECTION

When Princess Diana got her entry into the next life, there was little mention of the drinking beforehand. There was no discretion exercised here, but the driver did survive and we did have the "chaser": a coroner's inquest. *Could that happen to me?* we wonder. Many of us proclaim we truly drive better after we have a few drinks. Ha!

AFFIRMATION

O Lord, let me not be one of the arseholes who thinks he can drink and drive!

July 22

> Holding on to anger, resentment,
> and hurt only gives you tense muscles, a headache,
> and a sore jaw from clenching your teeth.
> Forgiveness gives you back the laughter
> and the lightness in your life.
>
> —Joan Lunden

REFLECTION

It is also said that harboring a resentment is like taking poison and waiting for the other person to die. A resentment is akin to giving another human the limitless gift of power over my emotions.

AFFIRMATION

May the bowels of my resentment apparatus be wide open today and all the days of my life.

July 23

Even though a number of people have tried,
no one has yet found a way to drink for a living.

—Jean Kerr

REFLECTION

No, Mr. Wise Guy. Wine tasters do *not* drink: they taste and spit it out and go on to the next glass. Many of us have succeeded in drinking for the *opposite* of a living, i.e. "a dying," and still without any pay or pension.

AFFIRMATION

Sober, I will stay longer above ground and remain in better health to explore this lovely world around me.

July 24

The supreme vice is shallowness.

—Oscar Wilde

REFLECTION

Groucho said, "The most important attribute is sincerity. If you can fake it you've got it made." That kind of shallowness is dismissive. It refuses to acknowledge the sanctity of the individual and eventually it comes home to roost in painful ways. People have built in bull-detectors. Sincerity and honesty are the best means of achieving your goals. There are no short cuts even when you find a sucker.

AFFIRMATION

Help me to bring myself entirely to my life, to be there for those I love, and to give help where it is needed.

July 25

> My most constant temptation—
> the one against which I never stop fighting
> to the point of exhaustion—
> is cynicism.
>
> —Camus

REFLECTION

What is it about cynicism that is so appealing? Well, it consists of a delicious combination of self-righteousness, victimhood, superiority, and disdain. It is a declaration that evil will always defeat good and an "I told you so attitude" that refuses to take responsibility for one's life and cedes all power to the triumph of the negative. It also sounds like a dry drunk.

AFFIRMATION

Help me to understand that cynicism is belief in the negative. I pray that I may always be aware of my propensity for self-pity.

July 26

> One clever lad's definition of "steam" is:
>
> "Water that's gone mad with heat."

REFLECTION

It's apparent that all beverages have water as their main ingredient. In small quantities, it's a profound and wonderfully healing liquid. It cleans, it purifies, it quenches thirst and does wonders for our insides. Then we add fermented grains, grapes, or berries, and we create a tempest in a tankard and we are left with mere wreckage. When will we ever learn? When will we *ever* learn?

AFFIRMATION

Water is also sometimes called "Adam's Ale," and a pint of that will do for now, thank you.

July 27

> What happens to a dream deferred?
> Does it dry up like a raisin in the sun?
> . . . Or does it explode?
>
> —Langston Hughes

REFLECTION

A dream is like a vision—it is God's way of showing us what his will for us is. And yet we all seem to have a difficult time accepting our dream and letting ourselves do what is necessary to achieve it. The most profound question will always be: Can I allow myself to be happy by following my dream? Or does my dream remain deferred in rationalizations and excuses? If that is the case, then there is always the possibility for that "explosion"—that moment when we can no longer hide the truth from ourselves. It can either break us or lead us to freedom. Disney World is a lousy excuse for reality.

AFFIRMATION

I know that I must always be true to God's will for me. There is no way to escape it.

July 28

> Sooner or later, false thinking
> brings about wrong conduct.
>
> —Julian Huxley

REFLECTION

False thinking is another way of describing self-deception. There are just a few who can be said to have never indulged in the practice. No one has ever met them but the rumor still persists. Living in reality is difficult for everyone and often we find ourselves fudging it or changing it to our liking or even accepting our wrong thinking. Ultimately it catches up with us. This is not about punishment. It is about not making life more difficult than it is. Check your thinking with your sponsor or someone else you respect and trust. It is hard sometimes for us to see our flaws even when we are absolutely sure we are right.

AFFIRMATION

Help me to be alert to my own propensity for self-deception. Help me to understand that when I'm living on the edge it is very easy to fall off.

July 29

> I never heard praise ascribed to a drunkard
> but that he bears his liquor well,
> which is a better commendation
> for a brewer's horse.

REFLECTION

It's odd what pride we take in being praised for being complete idiots. Such praise comes from dwellers of slimy pits, who fear one of their number will find the light and leave.

AFFIRMATION

Let me always be aware of the difference between praise and flattery, so that I may not be prideful of my character defects.

July 30

> There is no drinking after death . . .

REFLECTION

Some of us are convinced that death is a release from our obsession. However, nearly all obsessions are transient, and death is quite permanent, so it behooves us to give life a chance.

AFFIRMATION

Knowing I have at least one day in my life that I can contribute to the good with my presence, I'll give it a go today.

July 31

> It is only with the heart that we can see rightly.
> What is essential is invisible to the eye.
>
> —Antoine de Saint-Exupery

REFLECTION

The poet John Keats said that all intelligence comes from the heart. Life is not about brains but about vision. It is often like playing blind man's bluff with our eyes wide open. It's not about things being black or white or two plus two equaling four. It's about nuance and reading between the lines. We have to listen to that place in the gut that is very close to the heart. That small voice that speaks without words but says, "Ah ha." It is the inherent good in our nature that asks us to listen—and to see.

AFFIRMATION

I realize that the truth always exists within me. Help me to always listen to my heart, the place where God dwells in me.

August 1

> We understand more than we know.
>
> —Pascal

REFLECTION

We all carry the truth inside of us. It is given to us the day we are born. Somewhere along the way it gets lost and we forget that we ever had it but it is there inside of us. Finding it is the quest of our spiritual journey, finding the mystery that is within all of us.

AFFIRMATION

I know that the truth is within me. And I know that understanding comes from the heart not the head. God has stamped me with his own seal of approval.

August 2

It is easy to live for others, everybody does.
I call on you to live for yourself.

—Ralph Waldo Emerson

REFLECTION

There is a huge difference between enlightened self-interest and pure selfishness. We learn in the program that we have to set ourselves right before we can really be there for others. This is a fact. Doing the right thing for ourselves is something that many of us have a hard time with because we were never taught that it is the first requisite for personal freedom and success. As the old saying goes: Charity begins at home.

AFFIRMATION

Help me always to be true to my myself. I know that when I do what's best for me, I do what's best for everybody.

August 3

> The past in many ways is
> just as mysterious as the future.
>
> —Claude Colville

REFLECTION

The past can inspire us just as easily as it can bedevil and deflate us, holding us captive to a history we can never change. It is uncanny how members of the same family can have such different perspectives on so many similar experiences. But that is the mystery of the past. It is a highly individual element in our lives but it still has to be viewed through the reality of today and our ability to begin to see things differently in our sobriety.

AFFIRMATION

I pray that the past may not be a burden to the present. Help me to see where I have been, and where I am going, sure in the knowledge that looking forward or looking back, God has a plan for me.

August 4

> Too long a sacrifice
> can make a stone of the heart.
>
> —W. B. Yeats

REFLECTION

It is so easy to develop a martyr complex. To put everything and everyone ahead of ourselves and then feel deprived or put upon. Then we allow ourselves to believe we are being taken advantage of. The truth is that no one is holding a gun to our heads, forcing us to act as we do. When we sacrifice or put ourselves out for others it can only be done freely, with no expectation of a return or a reward. Don't give any situation or act the power to turn your heart to stone.

AFFIRMATION

Help me to understand that the only soul I can save is my own. To know that I can't get anyone sober and I can't get anyone drunk.

August 5

> Whoever has lived long enough
> to find out what life is knows
> how deep a debt of gratitude we owe to Adam,
> the first great benefactor of our race.
> He brought death into the world.
>
> —Mark Twain

REFLECTION

It is in avoiding the thought of death that we embrace the substance that murders us emotionally, spiritually, and physically. We become fearless in the face of all that frightens us, a condition that lasts 'til we wake up in fear and trembling once again.

AFFIRMATION

If I can accept my own death and know its inevitability, then I can get on with my life today.

August 6

She was only a moonshiner's daughter,
but he loved her still.

REFLECTION

As a heavy drinker, I never valued my fellow humans. I only saw ways to use or misuse them. As a sober alcoholic, I once again know men, women, and children as God's creatures.

AFFIRMATION

Today let me see the Higher Power in every man, woman, and child I meet.

August 7

> Selfishness is the only real atheism.
>
> —Israel Zangwill,
> *Children of the Ghetto*

REFLECTION

Selfishness contains within it all of the worst traits we are capable of having. It puts the self ahead of everyone else, perhaps even God. It may smile and even be gracious, but its terms are always that it be recognized as being more deserving, more entitled, and more worthy than anyone else. And at its center there is nobody home. Like the eye of the hurricane or the hole in the doughnut—nothing, because all it can see is itself.

AFFIRMATION

I ask for the gift of charity. I hope that I may always be aware of the world around me and be able to respond to the needs of others.

August 8

> Solitude is as needful to the imagination
> as society is to the character.
>
> —Robert Lowell

REFLECTION

Without imagination we could never progress. It is the gift God has given us to allow ourselves to see what is possible and what we are capable of. It has to be nurtured in solitude. That doesn't mean sitting in an empty room or locking yourself in a cabin. It can be a walk through the park or along the banks of a river. It can be any place where we can turn our conscious minds off and let our unconscious emerge. It is just as true that our characters cannot be formed in a vacuum. We must be engaged as fully as possible in the process of life and the exchange of experience and knowledge with others.

AFFIRMATION

I know that my imagination is the most precious gift that I've been given. Help me to nurture it and to act out of it.

August 9

> There is no bone in the tongue,
> but has often broke a man's head.
>
> —Irish proverb

REFLECTION

The defensive alcoholic believes in the devastating offensive strategy. He has to point out the defects of character in family and friends, lest the light fall on his own defects. Not alone does he feel it his bounden duty to let people know their faults, but it's necessary to broadcast them to all and sundry.

AFFIRMATION

I need only think before I speak, lest Evil snake its way past my tongue.

August 10

A little learning is a dangerous thing.

—Alexander Pope

REFLECTION

Sometimes we know just enough to get us into trouble. This is when we take ourselves into situations where we assume we know more than we do and, as a consequence, find ourselves exposed and our reputations tarnished. We are seen as one of those who knows less than he should. Be thorough in all of your endeavors, especially in learning. Know your subject cold—don't rush in where angels fear to thread unless you *know* the answers. Winging it is a dangerous proposition.

AFFIRMATION

Help me, dear God, to know my limitations. And help me to be prepared when opportunities arise. Help me to be honest in all of my dealings.

August 11

> Anger is rooted in our lack of understanding
> of ourselves . . . in desire, pride,
> agitation, suspicion.
>
> —Thich Nhat Hanh

REFLECTION

My immediate response to that statement? Bullshit! If someone does something rotten to me, I have a right to be pissed off! Right? Right! Then, what do I do? Sentence him to death? As a drinker, my judgment is impaired, so I elevate myself to judge over all of mankind. But, in doing so, I in fact condemn myself, thus giving my enemies total power over me. I am angry only when I'm afraid.

AFFIRMATION

I don't want to have the power of anger over anyone today, nor do I want anyone to have that power over me. Let me shine a light into the darkness of anger and let it be known to me.

August 12

George was determined that he would forego
his evening visit to the pub. He had to pass it
on the way home, so with gritted teeth
he strode determinedly past the beckoning door.
Fifty yards down the road,
he congratulated himself with,

"Good man! You've done it!
Now, let's have a drink to celebrate Willpower!"

REFLECTION

If that is not an example of alcoholic rationalization, spiced with dollops of insanity, we'd wonder what is. Sometimes we mistake good intent for the deed itself, and are quite happy at our goodness, but then we're astonished when we wake up to find we'd "done it again."

AFFIRMATION

When I get past it, O Lord, let me quicken my step so that I'm far from it.

August 13

> Drinking too much ain't bad;
> it's alright letting yourself go,
> as long as you can let yourself get back.
>
> —Mick Jagger

REFLECTION

If I get in a barrel to go over Niagara Falls, and I do it sober, I may be foolhardy, but that's a risk I chose. However, once the barrel and me start dropping, there is no return, and the outcome is uncertain. I may survive, but . . . The outcome is just as uncertain with that first drink.

AFFIRMATION

O God of Risks, keep me out of barrels, bottles, flasks, or any other spirituous containers just for today.

AUGUST 14

No man can be proficient at drinking.
If a man tells you he has mastered
the hallucinatory effects of whiskey,
you can be sure it's the whiskey talking.

—John B. Keane

REFLECTION

There is nothing sillier and, conversely, deadlier, than whiskey babble. The stupid, disconnected thought is given a voice and some things are said which will never be forgiven.

AFFIRMATION

If I'm not moderate in my speech this day, then let me be blissfully silent.

August 15

> Whiskey is no doubt a devil . . . but why
> so many worshippers?

REFLECTION

The one thing whiskey always looks: sober in a glass. It looks settled, has a nice aroma (or "bouquet," as fatuous wine sippers say), and doesn't attack unless invited into the entrails. It becomes a devil only through the black magic of humankind.

AFFIRMATION

I'll acknowledge all alcohol today, and leave it to others to enjoy.

August 16

If you can't have faith in what is held up to you
for faith, you must find things to believe in yourself,
for a life without faith in something
is too narrow a space to live.

—George E. Woodberry

REFLECTION

I can't see the wind, yet I know it's there. I can't see electricity, yet I know its power. Whether I like it or not, and scoff as I may, I must have faith that there are powers greater than me moving mountains and men's minds.

AFFIRMATION

Today, let me put aside my human weaknesses and accept on faith that which I don't really understand.

August 17

> Forgiveness is almost a selfish act
> because of its immense benefits
> to the one who forgives.
>
> —Lawana Blackwell,
> *The Dowry of Miss Lydia Clark* (1999)

REFLECTION

Forgiving is not merely giving absolution to those who have injured me. It is an active cause in that, as best I may, I might help those who hurt and injure to reverse their actions and so be helpful to humanity.

AFFIRMATION

By my example this day, let me help another human being to see the light.

August 18

What's the difference
between a stagecoach driver and a bartender?

As a rule, the stagecoach man has to look
at only six of them at a time.

REFLECTION

A horse's ass merely follows the horse's head, and rapidly moves away from any shit deposited, whereas the alcoholic goes around in circles, constantly wallowing in the detritus of his own life.

AFFIRMATION

Today, I will lift my head, look toward the light, and one step at a time I will begin my sober journey.

August 19

> Nearly all drugs have side effects,
> such as the sudden death of the patient.
> Alcohol is the same,
> only it takes a little longer.
>
> —Philip Mason/Malachy McCourt

REFLECTION

We forget that alcohol is a drug and can be beneficial, if you're not allergic to it. For some, it has side effects; for others, it has full effects, and many of us know when it's "full" time.

AFFIRMATION

If I don't know by now what the stuff does to me, let me seek treatment at once.

August 20

Do be my enemy, for friendship's sake.

—William Blake

REFLECTION

It's the nature of the disease that it urges its victim to turbulence and excitement—any extreme will do. Be it obsessive love or raging enmity, the disease sez: "I'll be your friend or anything else you want me to be."

AFFIRMATION

A couple of deep breaths, a kind thought, and the serenity of prayer should be a good start to my day.

August 21

> Drinking makes such fools of people
> when people are such fools to begin with.
> It's compounding a felony.

REFLECTION

Ignorance of the law is no defense in a court of law, but ignorance of the laws of nature may explain some of our self-destructive behavior.

AFFIRMATION

May I find the knowledge and the wisdom to compound the joy of the child with my own.

August 22

Alcohol taken in sufficient quantities produces
all the effects of intoxication.

—Oscar Wilde

REFLECTION

Now, there's a novel idea! Fancy drinking to the point of intoxication! That clever notion pops into the head just about any day of the week, at any hour. 'Twould be wise not to entertain it, as it gets more reasonable the longer we ponder it.

AFFIRMATION

This day being a good one, I'll decide to live it sober.

August 23

> Hail, charming power of self-opinion,
> For none are slaves in thy dominion,
> Secure in thee, the mind's at ease,
> The vain have only one to please.

REFLECTION

Again, we find the strange bedfellows of grandiosity of mind and sewer self-esteem. There is no balance in our lives when we are caught in our see-sawing ego trips. There is no peace then either.

AFFIRMATION

Whatever I think of myself today, let me simply do my best and not think either of success or failure.

August 24

> They never taste, who always drink;
> They always talk, who never think . . .

REFLECTION

When I drink, it's not for the taste—it's for the effect, and I'll not waste time savoring aged whiskeys, wine bouquets, or cooling brews, when a fearful being inside is clamoring for surcease from some pain, real or imagined. After I drink enough, then I talk. My opinion doesn't matter, only the injunction. "I will not drink."

AFFIRMATION

Today would be a good day to abstain from alcohol, and today would be a good day for thoughtful words.

August 25

> The bottom of a whiskey bottle
> is always too near the top.

REFLECTION

The eyes and minds of us alcoholics are not made to normal human specifications. Our disease infuses us with fear of the scarcity of that poison we not only want but need.

AFFIRMATION

Today, let me not care if whiskey bottles are half full or half empty, so long as I'm filled with grace.

August 26

> He who sows hemp shall reap hemp;
> he who sows beans will reap beans.
>
> —Chinese proverb

REFLECTION

That's the way of nature, of life, of health, of disease. If we keep smoking cigarettes, we will reap lung disease. If we are alcoholics and keep drinking, then, of course, we will reap disaster.

AFFIRMATION

If I keep sowing wild oats, then it's a dead life I'll have. Let my tame sowing begin this today.

August 27

We must love one another or die.

—W. H. Auden

REFLECTION

It is all no more complicated than that. Simple, yet it is so difficult to love when it seems there are so many reasons not to. So natural to hold resentments, to judge, to feel victimized, to let envy blind us, and to have fear be the prime motivator of our actions. A paradise for quacks, madmen, dictators, and racists. Love is always waiting to come to us, and as soon as we can see beyond our own fear, it will embrace us. There really is nothing to be afraid of.

AFFIRMATION

Help me not to be afraid of love. Help me to understand that when I can love I eliminate fear.

August 28

If you would cure anger, do not feed it.
Say to yourself: "I used to be angry every day;
then every other day; now only every third
or fourth day." When you reach thirty days,
offer a sacrifice of thanksgiving to the gods.

—Epictetus

REFLECTION

There are numerous new names for conditions that have existed for time immemorial, i.e. road rage, air rage, etc., and the courts are recommending courses in "anger management." A person with a spoon can do more with a typhoon than anger management can do for anger. What we need is "anger disposal," as in "waste disposal."

AFFIRMATION

Anger is a total waste of my time. Let me wrap it up and drop it in the trash as quickly as possible today.

August 29

I can't go on—I won't go on—I'll go on.

—Beckett

REFLECTION

Sometimes it feels like we're running on empty and we have no money for gas—and there's a posse behind us. And sometimes we ask ourselves if this sobriety business will ever get us anywhere. You get the whiff of a gin mill and you realize you have no money. Might as well go to a meeting. And you make it through another day. That's the way the program works. Sometimes our lack is God's grace working in our lives.

AFFIRMATION

Help me realize that all I have is today. And it's all I need to deal with. Help me to reach out when I need to. And to know that I can't do it alone.

August 30

> My dear child, you must believe in God
> despite what the clergy tell you.
>
> —Benjamin Jowett

REFLECTION

We are all entitled to our own take on God and religion. The main thing to keep in mind is not to reject without prior investigation and respect the views of others. But as has been pointed out, there is a very thin line between saints and madmen, and sometimes we can't tell the difference. The spiritual journey is a lonely one. No one can do it for you and there are no short cuts. It is strictly between you and the mystery.

AFFIRMATION

I have to let go of all of the old notions of a punishing God and a bad child. I have to learn to be there for myself and join my hand to God's.

August 31

> We may understand the cosmos but never the ego;
> the self is more distant than any star.
>
> —G. K. Chesterton

REFLECTION

Knowing ourselves is probably the most difficult task of all. We are really adept at hiding from ourselves as well as others, and we are also fantastic actors. How we convince ourselves that we are indeed the character we portray to the world. But the fact of the matter is we always know the truth. No matter how hard we try there is always that small voice of our true selves we are so reluctant to let ourselves hear. It may take a lifetime to really know ourselves. In fact that's what the journey is really about.

AFFIRMATION

I pray that I may seek my true self and become the person God intended me to be.

September 1

> I claim not to have controlled events
> but confess plainly that events
> have controlled me.
>
> —Abraham Lincoln

REFLECTION

It's been said in the rooms that even God can't operate in the future. Even He has to let process do what it has to. But we in our infinite wisdom take it upon ourselves to make sure that it turns out exactly the way we want it to, and when it doesn't we turn on God and demand to know what He is up to. Even our leaders with all of their power are just as powerless as we—and thank God.

The only thing we can control is our attitude and our response to situations as they arise. Lincoln was not a religious man but he believed in ultimate good and was undeterred in his determination to succeed. Setbacks forced him to call on aspects of his character he wasn't sure he had. It is the same with us. Life is always asking us to look deeper as it unfolds around us.

AFFIRMATION

Help me to understand that by recognizing my powerlessness I am given strength.

September 2

> First lady:
> "If I have another drink, I'll be feeling it."
>
> Second lady:
> "If I have another drink,
> I won't care who is feeling it."
>
> —Dorothy Parker

REFLECTION

There's the scenario for a sexual assault. Alcohol makes us feel all powerful. No drunk under the influence recognizes the sanctity of another's body.

AFFIRMATION

Today is a good day to remember that, though there are spare parts, we each have the one body only—may it be nurtured by me and respected by others.

September 3

All our resolves and decisions are made
in a mood or frame of mind
which is certain to change.

—Marcel Proust

REFLECTION

There is a time for making decisions in our lives and a time for making resolutions, but the most important factor in this process is achieving emotional balance before we decide on a course of action. Acting out of anger, envy, or that other well-known favorite, "victimhood," can only lead to very painful situations. It is really important to always check in with a mentor or sponsor before acting on raw, gut feelings. It is the same thing as making that call BEFORE you pick up the drink. Emotional sobriety is the greatest achievement of all.

AFFIRMATION

Help me always to pause and reflect before I act. Help me to always be aware of my emotional state and to not act precipitously.

September 4

> To be a spiritual person
> is not to be afraid of responsibility.
>
> —Rabbi David Hartman

REFLECTION

To be afraid of responsibility is to be afraid of life. We run in fear that we can't handle it and we are literally running from ourselves. Fear is the demon which separates us from our Creator and tells us we are not good enough. When we know we are connected to the divine, then our unnatural fear evaporates and we revel in our responsibilities.

AFFIRMATION

Help me to feel your presence in my life each day, dear God. Take my fear and all that separates me from you. Help me to revel in the gift you have given me.

September 5

> Whoever tells the truth
> is chased out of nine villages.
>
> —Turkish proverb

REFLECTION

Offered the choice between truth or a palatable poison, we'll most likely swallow the poison. Some of us say, "What's wrong with having a drink or two? It's the only bit of comfort left me in this tormented world." Not alone is the truth chased out of one village after another; it is chased out of many heads as well.

AFFIRMATION

If I can serenely say, "Good morning, Truth, and it's welcome you are," it will be a good day.

September 6

> Relationships are not always
> preserved in alcohol.
>
> —Anonymous

REFLECTION

Body parts, perhaps, but not the whole live body. Don't we rehash old hurts when we get drunk? And no matter how long after, don't we seek redress with long-distance calls in the wee hours of the morning? Alcohol can preserve insanity in its most potent form.

AFFIRMATION

May all my relationships, with family and friends, be not built on a liquid foundation.

September 7

> Drunkenness sets a man back
> in the esteem of people
> whose opinions are worth having.
>
> —Mark Twain

REFLECTION

Many of us doubt the possibility of being good and decent human beings, due to past deprivations and humiliations, so we hold in low esteem those who recognize or praise our best qualities, thinking they must be mentally deficient to think anything good of us.

AFFIRMATION

May I learn to value the esteem and respect of those generous enough to bestow them on me.

September 8

> Champagne is like a woman of the streets—
> always within reach, and its price
> is out of proportion to its worth.
>
> —Frank Harris

REFLECTION

To an addict or alcoholic, the champagne, despite its bubbly allure and festive associations, is still a toxic substance, just as patronizing the street lady is toxic to a marriage.

AFFIRMATION

Soap bubbles will be festive enough today, and let me pray for the woman of the streets.

September 9

> One thing alcoholic folks have
> in common with monarchs
> is the right to use the royal "We."
>
> —Malachy McCourt

REFLECTION

As Queen Victoria often remarked, "We are not amused!" I'd like to know which of her wasn't. It's not easy to think of this disease as a pulsating, living, fluttering entity, yet we accept that cancerous tumors are our own flesh and blood, growing and murdering us without our consent. Alcoholism is part of us, and yet can be stood in a corner and kept there, but it doesn't stop growing—unless we yank it out by the roots.

AFFIRMATION

If I can face this disease, I don't have to fight it. All I need is not to nourish it today.

September 10

> We are fighting Germany, Austria and drink,
> as far as I can see.
> The greatest of these foes is the drink.
>
> —David Lloyd George
> (British prime minister during World War I)

REFLECTION

He was talking to a nation that was attempting to drown its fear in drink. The enemy, drink, will always insinuate itself into any situation, be it defeat or victory.

AFFIRMATION

This day, O Defender, let me keep the enemy within without. Whiskey is the quisling that wants to bring me down!

September 11

> Drunkenness is temporary suicide;
> the happiness it brings is merely negative—
> a momentary cessation of unhappiness.
>
> —Bertrand Russell

REFLECTION

The alcoholic mind is filled with delusion. Pity me, as poor little me is, oh, so sensitive, and nobody understands how this rough, tough world brutalizes my delicate nature. Is it any wonder I have to drink to protect myself from the daily onslaught? "Poor me, poor me, poor me . . ."

AFFIRMATION

Let me take a good look at myself today, and let me take a good solid inventory, so that I can use all my gifts to make life enjoyable.

September 12

> I am, in plainer words, a bundle of prejudices
> made up of likings and dislikings.
>
> —Charles Lamb

REFLECTION

In other words, I'm fairly human. Like any humanly prejudiced being, I'm fairly certain that people are vastly and deeply fascinated by my dislikings and hang onto every prejudiced syllable. An exit poll would show they haven't heard a word I said.

AFFIRMATION

O Lord, keep me from sonorous expression of things that don't matter to my joy of life.

September 13

> The hatred you're carrying
> is a live coal in your heart—
> far more damaging to yourself
> than to them.
>
> —Lawana Blackwell,
> *The Dowry of Miss Lydia Clark* (1999)

REFLECTION

"Hate" is one of the most powerful and evil words in the language, yet it is used as casually as if it were "love." It can be spoken with impunity on television or radio, and yet there are other words we are forbidden speak which are puny in their implications. I know of nothing monstrous enough to deserve my hatred.

AFFIRMATION

Today, I will simply try to love that which is opposite of what I might think to hate.

September 14

> There was the alcoholic who had given up cigarettes,
> and six months later resumed smoking
> because he didn't want to become
> a slave to self-control.

REFLECTION

We often hear from red-nosed pundits that you can't trust a man who doesn't drink or smoke or bed down as many women as possible. Spoken as if addiction were an accomplishment rather than a disease—by those afflicted looking for support of their foolishness.

AFFIRMATION

O Divine Orator, keep me from stupid pronouncements and may I be able to tolerate those who make them.

September 15

> He would go to mass every morning
> if Holy Water were whiskey.
>
> —Irish proverb

REFLECTION

There is no one so "moral" as the drunk in denial. All around him the world is in chaos and on the low road to hell, and just because he takes a drink or two to quiet his nerves, everyone criticizes him. It is so hard to be holy and drunk, since knowing right from wrong whilst drunk is out of the question.

AFFIRMATION

May I recognize my hypocrisy this day and place it in the trash.

September 16

> The greatest pleasure I know
> is to do a good action by stealth
> and to have it found out by accident.
>
> —Charles Lamb

REFLECTION

We addictive folk are of the opinion that the sun shines out of our arse. "Self-centered" is too loose a definition when we are in the throes of our thirsts.

AFFIRMATION

Let me today, just for fun, do something good for somebody, making sure 'twill not be discovered even by accident.

September 17

Life is an incurable disease.

—Abraham Cowley

REFLECTION

Of course, we can view life that way if we are cynical. Or, we look at it as a lighted, challenging path to enlightenment. Whatever life is, however long, however short, I've got it and I do accept it.

AFFIRMATION

Today, I'll more energetically and creatively celebrate the life within and the life without.

September 18

> Stone walls do not a prison make
> nor iron bars a cage.
>
> —Richard Lovelace

REFLECTION

No one in their right mind would opt for a prison sentence they didn't deserve, yet so many of us put ourselves in jail every day. We convince ourselves it is not so bad and on some days even the food seems to have the touch of a gourmet hand. The fact is we are masters of deception—and we are the ones deceived. Our own feelings of unworthiness and our isolation from a loving God are our jailers. Our program is the key to freedom and leads us to a life well lived.

AFFIRMATION

God, show me the way out of my self-imposed prison. Help me to see beyond the limitations of my narrow view. Restore me to the freedom I was born with.

September 19

> I never give 'em hell.
> I just tell 'em the truth
> and they think it's hell.
>
> —Harry Truman

REFLECTION

Avoiding the truth is one of our most highly developed abilities and probably for good reason. It isn't always easy to bear and sometimes it hurts. But unless we face it we can never know any real peace or satisfaction. Clinging to fantasy is like being on a life raft with holes in it.

AFFIRMATION

God, help me not to be afraid of the truth. Help me not to hide in my illusions. Bring me into the light of reality no matter how painful it is.

September 20

> Customs officer, to a man returning
> from a pilgrimage to Lourdes:
>
> "What do you have in those bottles?"
>
> "Holy and blessed water from Lourdes."
>
> "Smells like brandy to me!"
>
> "Oh! Glory be to God! Another Lourdes miracle!"

REFLECTION

Covert drinking does as much damage as the open kind, and brings a greater burden of guilt. Who do we think we are fooling in our daily lives?

AFFIRMATION

Today, let me realize the only fool was me, and I have a chance to unfool me.

September 21

> The future is an opaque mirror.
> Anyone who tries to look into it
> sees nothing but the dim outlines
> of an old and worried face.
>
> —Jim Bishop

REFLECTION

No matter how we try, we cannot step into the future. I cannot drink tomorrow's drink or take tomorrow's drug or cuddle tomorrow's child. I can't get sober at tomorrow's meeting. Again, if you want to give God a howling laugh, tell him your future plans.

AFFIRMATION

If I can't deal with today, give me the grace to deal with the next five minutes.

September 22

> He that kills a man when he is drunk
> shall be hanged when he is sober.
>
> —Proverb

REFLECTION

Whether we kill someone, abuse someone, or assault someone, if we live, we shall have enshrined in our hearts a little bit of hell. We may never be forgiven for what we have done, but we can and must make the best amends possible.

AFFIRMATION

Today, I know that forgiveness may not be possible, but let me make amends to those I have hurt in the past.

September 23

> A lifetime of happiness! No man alive could bear it. It would be hell on earth.
>
> —George Bernard Shaw,
> *Man and Superman, Act I*

REFLECTION

One child said she would not like happiness all the time, because she would not be able to feel sadness and grief at the death of her grandfather. If happiness is a mature acceptance of all that is visited upon us in our daily lives, then that's for me.

AFFIRMATION

Life is what happens; just let me be there when it does.

September 24

> A saloon is the poor man's club run
> with intent to make him poorer.
>
> —Frank McKinney Hubbard

REFLECTION

If an alcoholic were astray in the Sahara, there is no doubt the next oasis would serve booze. Our disease is resourceful, and is not alone a capitalist but an equal-opportunity victimizer as well. The saloon is another well-placed tool of mass destruction for any and all alcoholics.

AFFIRMATION

Let me recognize that they, the ubiquitous "they," have the right to sell booze. I have the right to pass by, so we're equal.

September 25

> If all the tears that are caused by alcohol
> could be rained down on the earth,
> I am sure the whole of mankind
> would drown in the deluge.
>
> —Justie Lee

REFLECTION

There is hardly a person alive who would not subscribe to the above thought. So why do we have to be constantly reminded of the terrorism of booze? Because of the great ally of our disease, called "amnesia," which blots it out.

AFFIRMATION

My disease seeks election every day in my life. May my vote be for me and the good life.

September 26

> A self-pitying drunk was droning on to his friend about all that he suffered in his life.
>
> "I believe," he said, "I have suffered everything that man fears, except death, and I expect that I shall live to suffer that also."

REFLECTION

Nothing is too absurd for the "poor me" type of human being. The world torments us, and we try to appear "heroic," even though life is just doing what life does—to each one of us.

AFFIRMATION

Let me not sink into a self-pitying torpor. I need to take responsibility for my actions today.

September 27

The enemies of the Bodhisattva
are not common foes of flesh and bone—
they are inner delusions, the afflictions
of self-cherishing and ego-grasping, terrible demons
that catch living beings in a snare of confusion,
causing pain, frustration, and sorrow.

—Dalai Lama

REFLECTION

Our all-destructive disease will attack gods and anyone else in its path. The only defense is to step off the road and let it thunder by. Some folks believe it prudent to walk a bit of the road with the demon, but they soon find out that you cannot be in the company of Evil without being infected. That applies to those of us who think we can take one drink, one toke . . .

AFFIRMATION

I'll be happy today to know I need not walk with demons or obsessions or with fools who do.

September 28

> Everyone has talent but what is rare
> is the courage to follow it into the dark places.
>
> —Erica Jong

REFLECTION

Some of us are afraid of our own powers—the gifts and talents that God has given us. We find it hard to believe that "regular guys" like us could have talent. It is much easier to stand back and settle for mediocrity—that sinecure that leads to fat bellies and large asses. Our talents bring us to places and situations in which we may feel uncomfortable, even frightened. There are many who balk at taking responsibility for what they have been given; but to walk away from your own nature will only make life more difficult.

AFFIRMATION

I accept the gifts that God has given me. I want to take responsibility for them and make my contribution to the world.

September 29

> The ideal is in you
> and the impediment is in you too.
>
> —Carlyle

REFLECTION

There is only one aspect of life over which I have any control and that is my attitude toward it. Now none of us have achieved any kind of prolonged positive attitude. Many of us would be locked up if we had, and friends would avoid us. The thing is we have to work on it every day. Even in the midst of our negativity we can turn it around by a change of attitude. The real issue is: Do you want to change it? There is a perverse pleasure in negativity—self-righteous despair or that old favorite, "I told you so. Nothing ever goes right for me." Well, you can be sure that with a negative attitude it never will. We really do have a choice and we have to make it every day.

AFFIRMATION

Help me to understand that I have to make a commitment to the best that is in me every day of my life.

SEPTEMBER 30

> I shall pass through this world but once.
> If therefore there be any kindness I can show,
> or any good thing I can do, let me do it now.
> Let me not defer it or neglect it.
>
> —Etienne de Grellet

REFLECTION

Never pass up an opportunity to do something good, not because of what may accrue to you but simply because it was there to be done. Sometimes we feel that we are given too many opportunities. Time to give someone else a chance. And sometimes these seem more like obligations than opportunities. That is never the case. When we do good, we feel better simply for having done it. It is how God sends us his grace.

AFFIRMATION

God, help me never to pass up an opportunity to do some good or to help someone in need. Help me to understand that we are given a limited number of opportunities.

October 1

> Poison is in everything
> and nothing is without poison.
> The dosage makes it either
> a poison or a remedy.
>
> —Paracelsus

REFLECTION

Our emotions, when galloping out of control, are extremely toxic, particularly when we experience resentment. We need only to pull back the reins of control to find the poisoning hurt was not so great to begin with.

AFFIRMATION

May my hands be freed from carrying the burdens of resentment so that they will be open to the grace of forgiveness.

October 2

> There is nothing either good or bad
> but thinking makes it so.
>
> —Shakespeare, *Hamlet*

REFLECTION

It all boils down to attitude. How do I perceive the situation? Seeing disaster will surely bring it on, and yet sometimes even disaster can be the beginning of positive change. It is how we face what comes our way that is important. So many of us rush to label any situation or event. Our emotions—chiefly fear—fog our thinking and we tend to see things in black or white.

AFFIRMATION

Help me, dear God, not to be so quick to judge; to stand back and be objective. Help me to know that when I can keep you in the equation, chances are that all will be well.

October 3

Adversity introduces a man to himself.

—Sophocles

REFLECTION

The reality of life is that adversity will either pull us under or it will make us stronger. It presents us with the definitive way for us to find who we really are, and that is not always a discovery we are eager to uncover. But the truth is we are often surprised to find that we are far better than we thought we were. God has given each of us the ability to surpass ourselves. That process is the essence of spiritual growth.

AFFIRMATION

Help me to understand that adversity is also an opportunity for personal growth. Help me not to shy away from my problems or to bury my head in the sand. Help me to go toward adversity knowing that I am not alone.

OCTOBER 4

There is a time to keep silent and a time to speak.

—Ecclesiastes

REFLECTION

Exercising good judgment does not come easy to many of us. What is more satisfying than lashing out in a fit of self-righteous anger? Oh, that feeling of moral superiority. Oh, to be "in the right." *Please.* Emotional sobriety is a rare commodity and only comes to us from years of making asses of ourselves. Learning when to say something and when to be silent is the result of experience, self-awareness, and practice.

AFFIRMATION

Help me to understand the need for restraint of pen and tongue and also to learn to speak when the situation requires it.

October 5

The soul in essence will say to itself:
no one can build the bridge on which
you will cross the river of life—no one but yourself.
In all the world there is one specific way
that no one else can take but you.

—Nietzsche

REFLECTION

Now that is flattering and frightening at the same time. Yes—I really am special—but I still have to take responsibility for myself. When I think of all of the energy I've spent trying to get off the hook. I can't drive through life on somebody else's ticket. I have to find my own. It's the only one that will bring me through.

AFFIRMATION

God, help me to take responsibility for myself. Help me to be true to my own spirit. Help me to celebrate the gift of life which you have given me.

October 6

> I often joke that if you want to be selfish,
> you should be very altruistic.
>
> —Dalai Lama

REFLECTION

If we extend compassion and love to others, then it will come back in many ways. That is a paraphrase of "Cast thy bread upon the waters, and you will find it after many days." Most of us would deny being selfish vehemently, but in the case of the alcoholic in recovery, let it be.

AFFIRMATION

Today, let me find out the goodness of doing good deeds.

October 7

> Robert E. Lee came upon his army surgeon
> in front of a mirror, neatly tying his cravat
> while surveying intently.
>
> "You must be the happiest man in the world,"
> said Lee.
>
> "Why?" said the doc.
>
> "Because you are in love with yourself
> and you haven't a rival in the world."

REFLECTION

Aren't we the odd creatures? On the one hand, I've the most inflated ego in the universe, and on the other, I don't think I have any value at all as a human being.

AFFIRMATION

I'm as valuable as what I do in the way of good this day. Let me be willing, at least, to do it.

October 8

> Prudence must never be expected
> from a man who is never sober.
>
> —Cicero

REFLECTION

Drunks often seek prudence from each other, and lunatic counsel will seem like prudent advice. When the recipient of the advice wakes up in prison, 'tis rare for the dispenser of the counsel to be present for bail or any other help whatsoever.

AFFIRMATION

Let me know today if the source of my counsel is polluted.

OCTOBER 9

> My rule is always to do the business of the day in the day.
>
> —Arthur Wellesley,
> Duke of Wellington

REFLECTION

The business of any human's day is doing the right thing today. Yesterday is well gone and set in concrete, and tomorrow is not in my business plan, as I don't know if it will dawn for me.

AFFIRMATION

Today is my treasure. Let me enjoy full possession of it.

October 10

> One good reason for stopping the smoking
> of cigarettes and the drinking of booze
> is avoiding the tax, as opposed to evading it.

REFLECTION

Not the ultimate reason for getting out of bed in the morning sober, but it's a start.

AFFIRMATION

O Great Guide, even the smallest reason for avoiding that next drink is a boon to me.

October 11

> Belief consists in accepting the affirmations
> of the soul: unbelief, in denying them.
>
> —Emerson

REFLECTION

If I can accept the fact that I'm on this earth to be the best of what I am, and that my life is a gift of some divinity, then I'll have a go at actually being the best of what I am.

AFFIRMATION

Whatever the day drops in my lap, I'll handle it in the best way I'm able.

October 12

> Life's greatest happiness is to be convinced
> that we are loved.
>
> —Victor Hugo,
> *Les Miserables*

REFLECTION

Most of us are too embarrassed to confess to love of any sort. "Oh yes," we say, "I love the beach" or something inanimate like that, but humans, no. And we will be loath ever to say "I love myself" lest we send our friends running in hysterical confusion. What to do? Well, begin by loving yourself, and you don't have to tell anyone, and then think about all those you love, and then think on all those you suspect love you. That's a day's work.

AFFIRMATION

Let me begin my day with a loving inhalation, and then by saying "I love me and all I think I love."

October 13

A man said of his neighbor Powell:

"He is not like a Christian at all.
I have never seen him drunk."

REFLECTION

We always have to divert attention from our own doings. Pointing fingers is a refined alcoholic art form. We become wise—and sober—only when we quit blaming ourselves and others for our problems.

AFFIRMATION

If I can see myself today as I ought to be—sober, happy, joyous, and free—then I shall be happy, joyous, and free.

October 14

> Live in such a way that you would not be ashamed to sell your parrot to the town gossip.
>
> —Will Rogers

REFLECTION

So many of us, in the privacy of the home or hotel room, say to ourselves, "Who would know if I had just one?" "Just one," sez you to yourself, and the parrot says, "Just one . . ." Who would know, and who would care? That's disease jargon. In no time at all, the people you don't want to know will know all about it. Just one!

AFFIRMATION

The thought for the night is: "Just one more night of being clean and sober."

October 15

> One alcoholic had his toes amputated
> so he could stand closer to the bar.

REFLECTION

Some fellows only open their mouth to change feet. There is nothing that seems illogical to the alcoholic mind, so to get to the drink, what must be done must be done . . .

AFFIRMATION

O Lord, let me keep my toes if only to balance my life.

October 16

> An active alcoholic is like the miser who,
> when he died, left all his money to himself.
>
> —Anonymous

REFLECTION

There is none so selfish and self-centered as the drunk/addict in search of the bottle or the drug—so selfish that the thought of sharing a drink would bring on a withdrawal seizure. To be captive to any substance is simply slavery.

AFFIRMATION

I hope I may freely breathe air today and savor my life.

October 17

The first test of a man is his humility.

—Ruskin

REFLECTION

Humility is the understanding that without God I am nothing. I wouldn't even be here and I can never take credit for the gifts that He has given me, only the responsibility. The opposite of humility is to play God with my life and with those around me. This is called pride and it is the state in which we are almost sure to fall flat on our faces sooner or later.

AFFIRMATION

I pray to walk humbly through life, always aware that without the grace of God I am nothing.

October 18

> "Woodpeckers are more intelligent than you chickens," said the woodpecker.
>
> "Really," said the chicken. "Well, you seem to spend your days banging your head against a tree."
>
> "Ah," said the woodpecker, "have you ever heard of a Kentucky Fried Woodpecker?"

REFLECTION

We do have other ways of getting on with living besides banging our head on hard surfaces or getting fried. Sometimes doing nothing but sitting still will do just fine.

AFFIRMATION

Today is a good day to lend an ear to another suffering addict or alcoholic or any other human being.

October 19

Good is no good but if it be spend;
God giveth good for no other end.

REFLECTION

We ought never preach on the subject of another's addiction or disease. Mine own is enough to speak on, and, indeed, so is recovery. The blessings I enjoy today are in the nature of miraculous because the Creator has granted me one more day.

AFFIRMATION

Let me remember the gentle admonition: "You cannot keep it unless you give it away."

October 20

> I feel wine is a clog to the pen, not an inspiration.
> I cannot write after drinking even one glass.
>
> —Mark Twain

REFLECTION

That one drink, ever looming, threatens to sabotage the alcoholic's every dream and every endeavor.

AFFIRMATION

At the end of this day, I will be grateful that I didn't need the "Dutch courage" supplied by alcohol. My genius and creativity work only when unimpaired.

October 21

> I don't believe in dying. It's been done.
> I'm working on a new exit.
> Besides, I can't die now.
> I'm booked.
>
> —George Burns

REFLECTION

How many of us have listened to the lecture on the subject of killing ourselves with booze or drugs? Doctors, spouses, friends, children, lovers, and just about the whole bloody world is expert on the subject of my dying, and they never consult me! Just because I take a drink and my liver is like Bakelite, and I drive when I've had a few drinks, and my nose could be used as a stoplight, doesn't mean people can give me advice!

AFFIRMATION

If I can avoid being an asshole today, I'm on the way to being whole.

October 22

> I can take any amount of criticism,
> so long as it's unqualified praise.
>
> —Noel Coward

REFLECTION

As sensitive little alcoholics, we need to be boosted every day, not to mention every hour. If anyone criticizes us, it's cause for drinking, and if anyone doesn't praise us for being alive, it's cause for drinking. If someone looks at us, it's cause for drinking, and if they don't, it's ditto.

AFFIRMATION

O Lord, let me sing a song of life today, and of thanks for all I have.

October 23

Definition of "a writer's posthumous works":

"The books an author writes after he is dead."

REFLECTION

We dream, dream, dream, and procrastinate, and this cruel world will not get out our way while it torments us. Some day, we intend to do whatever we were meant to do, but in the meantime, what harm is there in a few drinks?

AFFIRMATION

I'll not have this day again, so at least let me begin the job, whatever it may be.

October 24

> For the error bred in the bone of each man
> and each woman craves what it cannot have,
> not universal love but to be loved alone.
>
> —W. H. Auden

REFLECTION

Maybe it is that basic instinct for survival that drives in us the craving to be loved alone. The idea of love being that if somehow we are not singled out for special attention, we won't get what we need. It is as though we believe that there just isn't enough love to go around. The reality is that we were not just created—but we were loved into existence. Love brought you here and love will bring you back to the Father.

AFFIRMATION

Help me to understand, dear God, that I was loved into existence and that your love is for all of us. No one is left out of your plan.

October 25

> Anger and hatred are our real enemies.
> These are the forces we need to confront
> and defeat, not the temporary enemies
> who appear intermittently throughout life.
>
> —Dalai Lama

REFLECTION

Because we are an obsessive kind of creature, it's easy for us to fixate on just about anything as the cause of our troubles. Anything will do: spouse, family, lover, boss, teacher, president, the weather, the job . . . fill in your own favorite here. We need to seek the true enemy, and to expunge it and replace it with love.

AFFIRMATION

Let me know mine enemy, so that I can stroll in the opposite direction.

October 26

There is no substitute for sober experience.

—Marty O'Farrell

REFLECTION

Recovery is a slow process. What causes us the most distress are the unreasonable expectations we have of ourselves. It took most of us a long time to hit bottom. To even begin to understand the physical and the spiritual process in living a sober life takes time. No matter how successful we were in our drinking lives we learn that in sobriety we are beginning a new life where the old experience is of little use to us. It is only in our sober lives that we gain in character and develop our spiritual lives. It all happens one day at a time for the rest of our lives.

AFFIRMATION

I pray that I may not make unreasonable demands of myself. Help me to be in touch with the pace of my recovery and to grow in sober experience.

October 27

Every man must get to heaven in his own way.

—Frederick the Great

REFLECTION

Or as the saying goes—there are many ways to skin a cat. There is no mass salvation. And no great movement which enlightens us all at the same time. No one sermon or tract can do it for us all. They may help open a door—but it always comes back to us and the countless ways there are to find God in our hearts. No one else can make the journey for you.

AFFIRMATION

I pray that I may make my journey through life with an open mind. Help me to be open to encouragement and help but to always know that my life is my responsibility.

October 28

> A good laugh and a long sleep
> are the best cures in the doctor's book.
>
> —Anonymous

REFLECTION

Can a drunk be funny? Yes, when he falls on his backside or flat on his side. Can he laugh? Yes, but he doesn't know why! Can he have a good sleep? Unlikely, as the demons then come out to play.

AFFIRMATION

I'll settle for a laugh or two today, and a good night's sleep tonight, which is more likely if I'm sober.

October 29

God and the Doctor we alike adore,
But only when in danger, not before;
The danger o'er both are alike requited—
God is forgotten, and the Doctor slighted.

REFLECTION

Most diseases need a dollop of faith in a higher power and the help of a healer. Because addiction, like diabetes, is always with us, we must needs say good morning to it, put it where we can see it, and live the day.

AFFIRMATION

Let me not be amnesiac when it comes to the disease, or ungrateful for the help I need this day.

October 30

> We live very close together—
> so our prime purpose in life
> is to help others.
> And if you can't help them,
> at least don't hurt them.
>
> —Dalai Lama

REFLECTION

We are all susceptible to the slings and arrows of outrageous fortune. There is so much of life that is totally beyond our control no matter how sincere our efforts or how worthy our goals may be. Sometimes it seems that the harder we try, the harder we get kicked in the butt. And that is why it is so important to be there for others. It takes the focus off us and lets our positive energy flow to those in need. This is truly how we find God in ourselves.

AFFIRMATION

It is important for me to be there for others. It is in losing myself in helping others that I find a light heart and a bright spirit.

October 31

Courage is resistance to fear—
    mastering fear—
    not eliminating it.

—Pascal

REFLECTION

Fear seems to be always with us in one way or another. There are times when it would overwhelm us if we let it. Knowing how to make our way never becomes routine. Each time we face fear, we have to draw upon our experience in recognizing it and finding in ourselves through God the ability to face it. Some fears are very real, even paralyzing, but we know that with the help of God and our friends, we will always find our way.

AFFIRMATION

I need you most when I am most afraid, dear God. I give you my hand and ask you to guide me through the swamp of my fear. Help me always to see you at the beginning and the end of it.

November 1

> The divine spark goes from God
> to the hand of man.
>
> —A. Whitney Griswold

REFLECTION

We all have the spark of divinity within us, like a microchip bestowed on us by the Creator. It is the direct connection to the mystery of the universe from which all of our greatest achievements derive. From Michelangelo to the discovery of DNA, each of us has a contribution to make. For most of us there will be no fame nor particular note made of our efforts, but all of us are necessary to the working out of God's plan.

AFFIRMATION

I am a vital and necessary part of the mystery of the Universe. God created me for the sole purpose of making his plan work. Help me to accept my place, dear God, and help me to realize there are no lead singers and no minor roles.

November 2

> The South is dry and will vote dry.
> That is, everyone sober enough
> to stagger to the polls will do so.
>
> —Huey Long

REFLECTION

When we see alcoholism as a moral issue or as a character defect, then we can use spurious laws to suppress or remove it, thus allowing hypocritical lawmakers the ego-swelling they feel is their due.

AFFIRMATION

O Great Physician, let me not dissect another's character until mine own is fully inventoried.

November 3

> It is our light not our darkness
> that frightens us the most.
>
> —Nelson Mandela

REFLECTION

So many of us shrink from the light of our own potential and hide in the darkness of that place where we are least ourselves. It is as if we believe that if we truly live who we are, then we believe we will be exposed as fakes. "Who are you to shine? Who are you to have the respect of your peers? Indeed—who says you are allowed to be happy?" As Satchel Paige used to say—you can run but you can't hide. When we put the booze down there is no more running. You are stuck with who you are and you will be amazed at how fantastic that guy is when you let your light shine.

AFFIRMATION

I am willing to let the very best of me come to the fore. I won't hide my light under a bushel.

November 4

> Man's greatness comes from his ability
> to overcome his condition.
>
> —Camus

REFLECTION

He wasn't talking about hangovers. It is about living. Bad things happen; good things happen; and sometimes it is hard to tell the difference.

Sometimes it seems that God has a weird sense of humor and we don't always get the joke. So laugh anyway, since there is very little we can control except our attitude. When we accepted our powerlessness over alcohol we began the process of accepting ourselves and the world as it is. This is the beginning of change.

AFFIRMATION

God, please help me to understand that it is only in recognizing my powerlessness that I can begin to see my life and my relationship with the world in a different light. Help me to know that those two imposters, success and failure, can only be measured by you. Help me to rise above the judgments of the world and to understand that it is only through you that I can overcome whatever the world may impose on me.

November 5

> Let not thy thoughts dwell upon the days
> of thy sorrows, but rather in those
> which brought thee thy peace.
>
> —Proverbs

REFLECTION

There are many regrets as we make our way along the journey but dwelling on them is an exercise in futility. Some of us are better than others at staying in the moment and concentrating on the positive. The only way to change the past is to change your attitude toward it; the best way to do so is to make the most of your life every moment.

AFFIRMATION

God, help me to understand that life is always a balancing act. Help me to be free of my own propensity for sadness. Help me to focus on the opportunities for joy.

November 6

> As the moth consumes a garment
> so doth envy consume a man.
>
> —St. Chrysostom

REFLECTION

There is no more destructive emotion than envy because it negates our own value as people. It totally rips apart the idea that, in God's eyes, we are all equal. It is also nearly always turned inward, causing us grievous harm, and it cuts us off from God's grace. And the kicker is that no amount of envy will change anything.

AFFIRMATION

I pray that I may catch envy in me before it can take hold. Help me to see you in everyone and in all circumstances. Help me not to deprive myself of the joy of seeing your grace made manifest in the happiness and achievements of others.

November 7

> All progress is precarious
> and the solution of one problem
> brings us face to face with another.
>
> —Martin Luther King, Jr.

REFLECTION

The great illusion is that we will reach a point in our lives where we will have figured it out, and from that point on it will be smooth sailing. It ain't fair and to date no one has figured it out. And if you meet the guy who is absolutely sure run like hell.

Experience shows that personal growth and maturity can only come from facing our problems, whatever they may be, and doing our best to resolve them. For us alcoholics there is no substitute for sober experience. Life will not leave us alone and trouble, when it comes, will not go away by ignoring it. Every situation is an opportunity for growth even if we go through it kicking and screaming. What a relief it is to realize just how imperfect we are.

AFFIRMATION

Help me to practice living one day at a time. All I have is this one day and if I live it well, God will take care of what's ahead of me.

November 8

> He who only drinks water
> does not get drunk.
>
> —Irish proverb

REFLECTION

So, what else is new? The founder of Alcoholics Anonymous, Bill Wilson, averred that most alcoholics are of above average intelligence. If that's the case, how is it we don't get it when told water won't make us drunk? As the man said, "Aye, there's the rub!"

AFFIRMATION

Let water be my wine this day, without any calculations.

November 9

Judge to Irishman:
"Where did you get the money for all that whiskey?"

"From my great and generous Scottish friend, MacTavish."

"Three months for perjury," says the judge.

REFLECTION

It's true some Scots make whisky and some Irish drink it, but the Irish don't have a monopoly on alcoholism, nor do the Scots have a monopoly on miserliness.

AFFIRMATION

My defects are human, not nationalistic. May I treat myself humanly today.

November 10

Too much drinking makes one
very improper for the Acts of Venus.

—Aristotle

REFLECTION

Booze may turn love to impotent lust, and thus to disappointment.

AFFIRMATION

May I be "guilty" of unconditional love, and no other kind, this very day, this very night.

November 11

> Always do sober what you said you'd do drunk.
> That will teach you to keep your mouth shut.
>
> —Ernest Hemingway

REFLECTION

There was a man who spoke from "experience," except he gained it all either while drunk or "not drunk" (which doesn't mean sober), so his "experience" was all delusional. Grandiosity is the hobgoblin of all us inebriates, and there isn't a thing we don't intend to do on the morrow, if and when we arise.

AFFIRMATION

O Lord, help me stay away from boastful and braggart societies, lest my braggadocio choke me.

November 12

> He had his beer
> From year to year;
> Then his bier had him.

REFLECTION

O, for a nice cooling draught of beer with a foamy head on a hot summer's day! Cool, yeah! But, the next day, *hell* is usually what awaits me.

AFFIRMATION

Today, let it be a cooling draught of water (no head needed, I've had enough of them!).

November 13

> Set up as an ideal the facing of reality as honestly and as cheerfully as possible.
>
> —Dr. Karl Menninger

REFLECTION

The three words in that quotation I like are "ideal," "honestly," and "cheerfully." Facing reality is an ideal, not an ordeal, and the honesty required lies in realizing that what is in front of us is what we have, and we ought to embrace it cheerfully. Such a situation would be ideal.

AFFIRMATION

It would be real today if I can be truly candid with one human being by saying "I love you," for example, and really mean it.

November 14

The bigoted, the narrow-minded, the stubborn,
and the perpetually optimistic
have all stopped learning.

—Philip B. Crosby

REFLECTION

Part of the disease is being close-minded and, in another sense, stupidly optimistic that one day alcoholics will have the pill that lets us drink without ill effect. In the meantime, we brood about what is being done to us by friends, family, and physicians. They actually want us to stop drinking! Ha!

AFFIRMATION

If I listen today with an open mind I can begin recovery.

November 15

> Drunk: when a person feels sophisticated
> but cannot pronounce it.
>
> —Irish witticism

REFLECTION

One apparent reason for drinking is fear. Fear of people, fear of insecurity, fear of nonacceptance, fear of reflection, fear of just not being good enough. There's nothing like a few stiff drinks to give us courage to face whatever. Alcohol is a false friend and will make life worse.

AFFIRMATION

Grant me the grace to see myself as a most acceptable human being.

November 16

Men do not drink for the effect it has on the body.
What they drink for is the effect it has on the brain.
If it must come through the body,
so much worse for the body.

—Jack London

REFLECTION

"Feeling no pain" is one of the euphemisms for drunkenness. Who among us, as drinkers and nondrinkers alike, has not witnessed a battered and bleeding drunk who seems oblivious to the injuries of his ravaged body?

AFFIRMATION

To the spare parts department in Heaven:

"There may be some replacements, but let me not forget that this is the only body I have, and as far as I know, we get one per person. Let me take care of it!"

November 17

> Is there anywhere a people more unsteady,
> more apt to discontent, than ourselves?
> Are we not of all people the most unfit to be alone
> and most unsafe to be trusted with ourselves?
>
> —William Congreve

REFLECTION

Humans are social creatures, and under the best of circumstances we need each other, for not all of us can weave clothing, build houses, grow food, heal the sick, and administer the law. We need to understand that isolation is not only selfish, but a symptom of a pernicious disease.

AFFIRMATION

At least today, let me greet another human being with an open ear. Having had my hearing restored, I can reenter society as a caring and giving human being.

November 18

Angry boss:
"You should have been here at 9:00 A.M."

Boozy employee:
"Why? What happened?"

REFLECTION

Most of us alcoholics and addicts do very precise calculations. We know the number of the street where the liquor store is on the corner, and where the drug dealer hangs. We know the opening and closing times, and how many ounces there are in a fifth, a quart, a gallon, or grams in a kilo, and we know how much each of these substance costs. Don't ask about shoes, bread, or rent—not important.

AFFIRMATION

Today is my day for counting blessings and valuing all that is true and worth loving in my life.

November 19

Always do what you are afraid to do.

— Emerson
(Counsel to a young person)

REFLECTION

Some of us are ashamed of our need to stop drinking. It's an admission of weakness, of failure, of being cheerless company, we think (the reality being that those who love us will cheer us on, while those who scoff will be dead long before us).

AFFIRMATION

Sobriety does not have to be trumpeted: it's "Thank you, I'll have an iced tea!"

November 20

Get your facts right first, then you can
distort them as much as you please.

—Mark Twain

REFLECTION

Most alcoholics won't deny that they drink. That's usually a fact that won't be denied. However, it's always accompanied by the "but," such as: "Yes, I drink, *but* I don't drink plum wine, sweet drinks, dark ale before 9 A.M., at church (except for communion), at funeral homes, or at temperance meetings, so I'm not an alcoholic."

AFFIRMATION

Let me take a shovel and see if I can get some of the bullshit out of my life, a shovelful at a time.

November 21

> Hell must be isothermal, for otherwise
> the resident scientists (of whom there must be many)
> could set up a heat engine to cool off a portion of
> their surroundings to any desired temperature.
>
> —Henry A. Dent

REFLECTION

The novice alcoholic does require civilized touches at the beginning of the drinking life. Cold beer, chilled white wine, icy martinis, and ice cubes in whiskey are all *de rigueur*. But as time and taste become more demanding, all these niceties go by the board and the temperature or the nature of the alcohol is no longer important.

AFFIRMATION

Hell is possible on earth; let me stroll around it.

November 22

> Extraordinary afflictions are not always
> the punishment for extraordinary sins,
> but sometimes the trial of
> extraordinary graces.

REFLECTION

Some of us are arrogant enough to believe we are shouldering more of life's tribulations than the ordinary citizen. 'Tis said plaintively, "God is testing me." Truth is, God (or Whoever) does not test anyone: you passed all the tests when you were born.

AFFIRMATION

Whatever is in the day ahead, let me delight in it, and if it be sad, let me cry, but let me be sober.

November 23

> There can be no real freedom
> without the freedom to fail.
>
> —Eric Hoffer

REFLECTION

In Dante's Inferno the most despised circle is reserved for those who have done nothing. The Devil can't stand them and God doesn't want them. They sat on the fence, never took a chance. To go forth, give your best, and then fail is to succeed gloriously. Thomas Edison, our greatest inventor, had thousands of failures, but he learned from every one. Those who are afraid to fail are never free. They are cut off from all of the infinite possibilities of life.

AFFIRMATION

Give me the courage to use the gifts and talents that you have given me. Help me to understand that the only failure is to let myself succumb to my fear. Let me experience the joy of achievement and success.

November 24

> Experience has shown us the enormous difference between piety and goodness.
>
> —Pascal

REFLECTION

Goodness knows no religion. It comes from that innate wellspring in us that responds to others as we would have them respond to us. It doesn't call attention to itself nor does it invoke anything higher than itself. It is wonderfully human. In contrast, piety somehow seeks to exclude the world and make a private party between God and itself.

AFFIRMATION

Let me be free from the idea that piety alone can suffice for the fulfillment of the spiritual journey. Help me to know that if I have not charity I have nothing.

November 25

> Anger causes open hands to close reflexively
> so that all grace and goodness are squeezed out.
>
> —Malachy McCourt

REFLECTION

If I allow it, my anger will be caused by people, places, or things. If I don't, then I have rendered them powerless over me and my emotions.

AFFIRMATION

Today, I'll smile and pass the slippery slopes of "justified" anger, righteous anger, or any anger whatsoever. Let me let it go.

November 26

The funeral of Queen Victoria was one
of the great events of the Twentieth Century,
and it took a large number of men
to carry the beer.

—British newspaper typo

REFLECTION

Queen Vicky would have been doubly unamused by that little glitch, because it took the "I" out of bier and left her with the draught.

AFFIRMATION

Would I like to be anyone but me, be it the king, queen, commoner, or star? Let me get out the abacus and add up my blessings today.

November 27

> Everyone speaks of happiness,
> but few know it.
>
> —Ruskin

REFLECTION

It would seem sometimes that the last thing we want in our lives is happiness. But when it comes to us, we can't beef, feel sorry for ourselves, or feel that we were born under a dark star. It really is hard to give all that up. Lincoln said that we are as happy as we decide to be. It's hard to have to see the truth in that. It would be much easier for us if it was all up to someone else. It's a lot like sobriety—no one can give it to you. You have to get it for yourself.

AFFIRMATION

Help me to understand that it is up to me to risk happiness. Help me not to be afraid of it.

November 28

Resolve to be thyself and know that
he who finds himself loses his misery.

—Matthew Arnold

REFLECTION

The hardest thing of all is simply to be ourselves. Who are you?

There is the guy that answers, "Go ask my mother." Chances are she has less idea than he has. Knowing ourselves is the beginning of a lifetime study. It doesn't come easy because it involves a lot of honesty, risk taking, and plain hard work. But the results are well worth it. Letting go of so many false perceptions is like knocking down the Berlin wall. You lose your misery, but with freedom comes greater responsibility because we can't blame our captors anymore.

AFFIRMATION

I pray for the willingness to let go of all that isn't me. I pray for the opportunity to achieve true freedom.

November 29

> The man who does not make mistakes
> usually does not make anything.
>
> —Edward J. Phelps

REFLECTION

The message here is very simple but still so hard to take in. Usually it is fear that prevents us from attaining our potential because we are afraid of failing. We become adept at snatching failure from the jaws of victory because the idea of success seem alien to our nature. So we try to stand still and get by, hoping no one will notice us. The one you can't escape from is yourself.

AFFIRMATION

Help me to revel in my failures, dear God, because they will lead me to my successes.

November 30

> Hell is the special favor of those
> who have asked for it insistently.
>
> —Camus

REFLECTION

Life will always throw us curves no matter how hard we try to do the right thing. Even if we live exemplary lives we will come to grips with bad breaks and situations that will seem to be grossly unfair. But no matter what happens, it is how we go through our difficult times that makes the difference. Attitude is everything. For some it will always be "I told you so. I'm just one of those guys who never gets a break. No matter what I do it always turns out the same." Sadly it appears that many of us create our own hell and then proclaim to all who will listen that we are victims. Captives is more like it. The worst hell is to be the prisoner of your own thinking.

AFFIRMATION

Being a victim is an entirely voluntary state. I pray that I may always know that.

December 1

> All human evil comes from this:
> a man's being unable to sit still in a room.
>
> —Pascal

REFLECTION

The devil we run from most often is ourselves. Sitting still and spending time with our demons is never easy, but if we can sit and not run, we may find that they are merely our doubts and the guilt we accumulate for real or imagined letdowns and failures. We judge ourselves very harshly even when God has long since forgiven us. The fact is our demons will never leave us. Sitting still and allowing ourselves to know them for what they are takes their power away.

AFFIRMATION

God, help me to know my demons. To see them for what they are: the hollow soundings of that dark side which work to separate me from you.

December 2

Breathing: "Breathing in, I see myself as still water; breathing out, I reflect all that is."

—Thich Nhat Hanh

REFLECTION

I cannot live on yesterday's breath or the hope of it tomorrow. Neither can I get high on yesterday's drink, on yesterday's drug, or tomorrow's connection for these same things. At every moment, I am just breathing life-giving air. And I know I'm living.

AFFIRMATION

No matter what, today I will allow one smile at least to light my face, and I will draw at least one very deep breath of gratitude.

December 3

> Humanity, I love you because you are hard up:
> you pawn your intelligence for a drink.
>
> —e. e. cummings

REFLECTION

Even the intelligent drunk will deny this; but the thinking equipment is gone, so the denial is without merit.

AFFIRMATION

I don't need to trade anything for my dignity, as one of God's kids.

December 4

It is sweet to drink but bitter to pay for it.

—Irish proverb

REFLECTION

If you don't understand that simple statement, you are paying dearly.

AFFIRMATION

Today, I need my mind and my money for service to humankind. Today, I must focus my mind and spend my treasure in service of mankind. With drink, both are utterly wasted.

December 5

> To show that they are not really drunks,
> some alcoholics will put up a show of propriety,
> such as wearing a tie at a nudist camp.

REFLECTION

We deny, we conceal, we play little games, we hide, blot out, lurk, skulk, and divert, so that no one will find out that we have the disease. There's a lot of creative energy goes into living a lie.

AFFIRMATION

Today, without excusing myself, just let me admit to being a victim of a disease.

December 6

> The best cure for seasickness
> is to sit under a tree.
>
> —Spike Milligan

REFLECTION

It's obvious that we don't get burnt if we don't stick a hand into the fire. I won't bleed if I don't slice my hand with a sharp knife. I won't get drunk if I do not go into a saloon and drink alcohol. I won't get drunk if I do not drink that first drink. Some of that stuff is too obvious for an alcoholic, but they do get decent funerals.

AFFIRMATION

The rules for staying alive can be repeated to me, all day, any day.

December 7

> If you don't learn to laugh at trouble,
> you won't have anything to laugh at
> when you're old.
>
> —Edgar Watson Howe
> (1853–1937)

REFLECTION

What passes for laughter in inebriated circles is either the bellow of a pained animal or the shrieks of a mob inflicting cruelty on a chosen victim. The best laughter comes at our own foibles, especially when we are the first to laugh.

AFFIRMATION

One laugh today will equal twenty-four hours of frowns. Let me have that one.

December 8

Any day above ground
is a good one.

REFLECTION

Alcoholism is the only disease to enlist our cooperation in our own destruction. It was incurable last year, today, and, far as we know, all coming days. But, joy of joys! Its remission is in our hands! The past is just that, and the future ain't mine, but today is in mine hands.

AFFIRMATION

Let me not take that first drink, so that one may be the best yet.

December 9

> The world is full of people whose notion
> of a satisfactory future is, in fact,
> a return to the idealised past.
>
> —Robertson Davies,
> *A Voice from the Attic*, 1960

REFLECTION

Nostalgia is a well-concealed evil worm. It absolves people from the responsibility of dealing with life as it is today and dealing with it on life's own terms. Today is the result of yesterday, and we had better be grateful for what it is and to clean up as much of the wreckage as possible—so that there will be less tomorrow if there *is* a tomorrow!

AFFIRMATION

Today is the only jewel in my collection. Let me treasure it.

December 10

> All I can say about life is,
> "Oh God, enjoy it!"
>
> —Bob Newhart

REFLECTION

There are sourpusses everywhere who insist that this life is a "vale of tears." It's logical that we were not put here to cry all the time, nor to laugh all the time, but there are days for just about everything. People die, people live, get born, get married, get jobs, get accepted to school, get dismembered and murdered in stupid wars, but, as the song sez, "That's Life."

AFFIRMATION

If I can't enjoy the day, may I endure it in the hope of a tomorrow.

December 11

> I don't know the key to success,
> but the key to failure
> is trying to please everybody.
>
> —Bill Cosby

REFLECTION

It's a well-worn fact that people-pleasing characterizes the addict/alcoholic. We fear being rejected or scorned, and many times are reduced to groveling or worse by violent speech or action.

AFFIRMATION

Today, even if I'm tempted to please anyone but my Higher Power, let me do the right thing.

December 12

> Speak to the devil and you will hear
> the clatter of his hooves.
>
> —Irish proverb

REFLECTION

If I entertain the devil in my head or home, there's a likelihood of his taking permanent possession. There's no point in fighting him; just don't ask him in, and the house and head will remain safe for my needs.

AFFIRMATION

Keep me off slippery slopes this day, so that I'll be reasonably happy for another twenty-four hours.

December 13

> When despair for the world grows in me—
> in fear of what my life and my children's may be—
> I go and lie down where the wood drake rests
> in his beauty on the water and the great heron feeds.
> I come into the peace of still water. For a time,
> I rest in the grace of the world and am free.
>
> —Wendell Berry

REFLECTION

It's all so simple (yet not easy) to take a deep breath and take comfort in the fact that the denizens of the natural world don't worry about the future. If the ducks and herons don't fret, why should I?

AFFIRMATION

I need to look at one star this night to know it's all right, right now.

December 14

"Is this man dangerously hurt?"
the alcoholic doctor was asked
as he attended the accident victim.

"Two of the wounds are fatal," he replied,
"but the third wound can be cured if the patient
will take a few weeks' rest."

REFLECTION

We don't know how many die from the ministrations of drunken doctors. Like members of any other profession, they have their percentages. May we never find one in our time of need.

AFFIRMATION

My disease is a self-diagnosed one, and my recovery is in the hands of the High Physician. May I find Her today.

December 15

In dreams begin responsibility.

—Pindar

REFLECTION

What you can envision and dream of accomplishing is the beginning of taking responsibility for your own life. Once the dream has come, do all in your power to bring it to fruition. When life's possibilities have been revealed, they are a manifestation of God's will for you.

AFFIRMATION

I pray for the courage to carry out God's will for me. Help me never to avoid or shirk action on what He has revealed to me.

December 16

> Half our lives are spent trying to find something to do with the time we spent rushing through life to save.
>
> —Will Rogers

REFLECTION

Time being neutral and without feeling, it just moves steadily ahead without interruption or detour. It's our perception of it that seems to speed it up or slow it. All I need to do is observe it and breathe deeply.

AFFIRMATION

Let my day be simply a measure of time well spent, without drug, drink, or despair.

December 17

> Dante places low in the Inferno
> those who willfully live in sadness.
>
> —Oscar Wilde

REFLECTION

There is a lot of sadness in the world but there is also a lot of happiness and joy. The fact is, if it were all sad, we would all still be crying in our beers. I don't think my eyes could stand it—all that salt—but there are those for whom sadness becomes a kind of addiction. There is a perverse satisfaction in acquired sadness, as if it were a mantle to be worn proudly. There is real pain and hurt but the idea always is to move on and grow through all that life has to hand us and not wallow in self-imposed martyrdom.

AFFIRMATION

Help me to move beyond the hurts and misfortunes I may encounter, and to know there is always a better day ahead.

December 18

> Here's to a temperance supper,
> With water in glasses tall,
> And coffee and tea to end with,
> And me not there at all.

REFLECTION

What self-demeaning alcoholic would be found at such a gathering? There would be talk, remembered talk, laughter and compassion, generosity, and no calls of apology the next morning for stupid behavior.

AFFIRMATION

Would that all my social gatherings were thus, but, in any case, my Higher Power is spirit enough at my table or at any feast.

December 19

> He who has a thousand friends
> has not a friend to spare,
> And he who has one enemy
> will meet him everywhere.
>
> —Ali Ibn-Abi-Talib
> *A Hundred Sayings*, 602–661 A.D.

REFLECTION

That which is our friend is oft presented in a stark, cold, clinical fashion. The dull, heavy clunk of the word "sober" hits the ear the way an indigestible lump of fatty meat hits the stomach. The enemy is attractive, seemingly alive, and oh, so alluring. As it has no gender, it's alluring to both man and woman, and oh, so beautiful. Haven't you noticed that in cigarette ads all the models have gleaming white teeth? "Sober" is always gray and seemingly lifeless.

AFFIRMATION

Let me sit back and take the fabric of my sober day and weave it into magic.

December 20

In our society,
we get to know each other over "drinks."
We associate feasts and celebrations with liquor.
We think we have to drink, and it is romantic,
as long as we can handle it.
For years I could,
and did, but it's misery
when we become addicted.

—Betty Ford

REFLECTION

It's knowing when we are addicted that is the problem. "What? Me? An alcoholic," we say. "Ha ha ha! I can stop any time I want to, not when some bluenose with no sense of life wants me to!"

AFFIRMATION

O Lord, let me be aware that today's devil is simply denial. If I'm alcoholic, let me know that I know it and make me take action.

December 21

> I have very poor and unhappy brains for drinking.
> I could well wish courtesy would invent
> some other custom of entertainment.
>
> —Shakespeare,
> *Othello*

REFLECTION

So much for the roistering heroes of Shakespeare's plays. Even the noble Moor had to recognize the power of booze. 'Twasn't enough that the poor man had to deal with the cunning and evil Iago!

AFFIRMATION

I will find good company today among people who have not pawned their intelligence.

December 22

> The beginning of love is to let those we love
> be perfectly themselves and not twist them
> to fit our image. Otherwise we love
> only the reflection of ourselves
> we find in them.
>
> —Thomas Merton

REFLECTION

True love, it is said, is really an act of the will, not something we fall in to. Many of us fall and then feel trapped and resentful that he or she is not what we thought them to be. Real love takes place in reality. And it is accepting and kind and uncritical. Try that on for size. It is not about changing anyone or having them do things our way. It is about letting them be who they are and loving them for it.

AFFIRMATION

God, help me to see beyond the romance and expectation into the reality of the human being.

December 23

> If I'm lucky enough to find a path to recovery,
> that's lucky enough.

REFLECTION

The wish, then:

> Deep peace of the running waters to you;
> Deep peace of the flowing air to you;
> Deep peace of the smiling stars to you;
> Deep peace of the quiet earth to you;
> Deep peace of the watching angels to you;
> Deep peace of the God of Peace to you.

AFFIRMATION

When I think I'm poverty-stricken, let me take the above inventory and know it's all free for the taking, making me rich beyond all dreaming.

December 24

> Gratitude is not only the greatest of virtues,
> but the parent of all others.
>
> —Cicero,
> *Pro Plancio I,* 54 B.C.

REFLECTION

In the parlance of the hip, if we drop the "gr" from "gratitude," we get an "attitude." In the current definition, "having an attitude" means "being angry and defiant," and that is very attractive to some younger folk. So, we have older people clashing with younger folk in the time-dishonored war between those who have lived and those with life still ahead of them. Neither is grateful for what the other contribute to society. The minuses are triumphant.

AFFIRMATION

Today, what do I have to be grateful for? Anything at all which I can hear, touch, and feel.

December 25

> The willingness to be happy
> is the closest we can come to God.
>
> —Thomas Merton

REFLECTION

Someone once said that we must risk joy. And for most of us being happy or joyful is a risk because we have never learned to trust happiness. In the movie *Tender Mercies,* Robert Duvall says, "I don't trust happiness—never did—never will." Most of us know exactly what he means. To simply endure without being open to the idea of happiness is not what God intended. So risk happiness. What do we have to lose but our misery.

AFFIRMATION

I pray for the courage to risk happiness, to trust in the gift of life, and to know that there is no downside to accepting all it has to offer.

December 26

Happiness is when what you think, what you say, and what you do are in harmony.

—Mahatma Gandhi

REFLECTION

In our society, happiness is often confused with being excited, celebrating, feasting, or doing anything which is not part of our daily routine. Dissatisfaction with what we do, with what we are, and where we are is exacerbated by advertisements which tell us we can be something other than ourselves if we eat things, use things, consume things, or work at something other than what we do, and so on. It's rare we are told about that harmony of thought, word, and deed as the key to quiet happiness.

AFFIRMATION

Let this be a reflective day for me, and may I be in harmony with all that's good for me.

December 27

> My happiness cannot possibly depend
> on my forcing changes on someone else.
> Nor does my misery come
> from anyone but myself.
>
> —George Bernard Shaw

REFLECTION

"If only they would do it my way life would be so much easier." It's amazing how we can let ourselves think like that, but as the lady said when she was watching the parade, "Everyone's out of step but my boy Johnny." Maybe it is only mothers who can display that kind of blind ego. Most of us can't afford to because it sends people running—and developing healthy relationships is out of the question. Even as we ourselves are the authors of our own egos, we are also the makers of our own misery. There has to be a better way.

AFFIRMATION

God, I pray for the gift of humility. Help me to see myself in all people. Help me to understand that the only person I can change is myself.

December 28

> There is more truth in honest doubt
> than in all the religions of the world.
>
> —Tennyson

REFLECTION

We have to learn to trust our own gut feelings despite the edicts and aphorisms and "you shoulds" of the pulpits. Honest doubt is part of the human condition and it is important to heed what our hearts tell us. We all embody God's truth and no one outside of yourself can give it to you. The trick is in learning to listen to it and recognize it when we hear it. That is our ultimate responsibility.

AFFIRMATION

Help me, dear God, to listen to your voice within me. Help me to trust it when it comes to me.

December 29

> The main thing is not to be afraid
> of being human.
>
> —Pablo Casals

REFLECTION

Being human means allowing ourselves to feel vulnerable, to live without pretense, and to let ourselves feel. It also means seeing ourselves in others and to have compassion and understanding for their pain and misfortune. There are no free rides in life. We all have to pay our dues. Those who console us may well be those we despised at another time. No one knows all the answers and most don't even know the questions.

AFFIRMATION

Help me to understand, dear God, that I am part of the human family, to know that you don't play favorites. Help me to dispel the idea that some are more equal than others. Help to put my humanity before my ego.

December 30

"I wish," said the drinker to the clergyman,
"that you had the keys to Heaven
so that you might let me in."

"'Twere better," said the clergyman,
"that I had the keys to hell
that I might let you out!"

REFLECTION

Life is not always delightful, having its share of dark days, but we can handle them if we don't exaggerate our troubles or pick up a "mood changer."

AFFIRMATION

The key to happiness should not be kept in a locked box: it's to be used every day.

December 31

> He who bends himself to joy
> Doth the winged life destroy;
> But he who kisses the joy as it flies
> Lives in eternity's sunrise.
>
> —William Blake

REFLECTION

The problem is that when it comes, we try to cling to joy instead of holding it lightly, knowing that it cannot stay with us for long. That is the nature of it, and if it appeared that we were joyful all the time they would take us away to dance with the guys in the white coats. Take it as it comes and be grateful that it stayed with you for a while.

AFFIRMATION

I am grateful for the gift of joy. Help me to take it as it comes from you, dear God.

INDEX

A
abstinence, 151, 237
abusiveness, 170
acceptance, 12, 14, 67, 127, 143, 164, 185, 285, 309, 345, 348
acknowledgment, 68, 88, 228, 252, 341
addiction, 141, 188
adversity, 277
advice, 104, 282
alcoholism as a disease, 19, 43, 51, 80, 102, 129, 135, 146, 165, 180, 184, 194, 253, 303, 326, 343, 349
amends, 24, 61, 266
amnesia, 269
anger, 28, 39, 90, 191, 224, 241, 330
anonymity, 37, 177

appearances, 116
appearances, keeping up, 340
attitude, 115, 273, 276, 310, 335
avoidance, 156

B
babble, 227
balance, 112, 127
blame, 150, 268, 287, 307
bragging, 173
breathing, 152, 337

C
calculations, 323
cause and effect, 239
champagne, 252
change, 113, 167, 202

charity, 31, 293
choice, 118, 183, 273
cleanliness, 9
coincidence, 92
compassion, 31, 280, 292, 304
consciousness, 153
consequences, 8
contentment, 7, 121
control, 245
courtesy, 21
criticism, 296
cynicism, 207

D
delusion, 271
denial, 35, 53, 70, 105, 136, 155, 165, 172, 195, 200, 201, 203, 205, 295, 319, 325, 355
dignity, 338
divinity, 306
doubt, 363
dreams, 209, 350
dry drunks, 50

dry vs. sober, 133

E
ego, 48, 60, 281
emotional sobriety, 90, 106, 247, 278
endurance, 36
enemies, 168, 254, 299
envy, 311
esteem, 251
evil, 176
extremity, 233

F
failure, 328, 334
faith, 62, 95, 115, 130, 229, 243
fame, 199
family, 134, 250
fear, 59, 126, 140, 248, 305, 308, 320, 324
flattery, 211
foolhardiness, 22, 111, 234, 258
forgiveness, 27, 230, 275
fraternity, 33, 187

freedom, 141, 262, 333
future, the, 107, 265

G
generosity, 274
God's plan, 117
good company, 353, 356
good deeds, 260
good intentions, 225
good works, 163
grandiosity, 316
gratitude, 21, 119, 137, 331, 359
growing, 18

H
hangovers, 98
happiness, 41, 73, 94, 267, 332, 360, 361
harmony, 361
hatred, 257
healthy thinking, 284
heredity, 71
honesty, 120
hope, 32
humility, 26, 291, 363, 364
hygiene, 175
hypocrisy, 55, 57, 259

I
illusion, 96
imagination, 99, 221
indispensable people, 11
individuality, 187
intemperance, 91
irony, 189
isolation, 4, 19, 145, 147, 322

J
joy, 158, 366

K
knowledge, 137

L
laughter, 101, 342
learning, 26, 52, 74, 223, 319
life, 261

loneliness, 42
losing, 54
lost time, 84
love, 45, 131, 240, 286, 298, 315, 357
luck, 193

M
madness, 46, 76, 131
maturity, 20, 65, 127, 33
mental health, 6
mistakes, 334
morality, 307
mortality, 29, 122, 148, 197, 212, 218

N
negativity, 47, 83, 103, 108, 149, 273
nostalgia, 344
now, 15

O
odds, the, 6
omnipresence, 114
one day at a time, 157, 28
opportunity, 78, 181, 274

P
pain, 30
past, the, 34, 85, 216
patience, 77, 278, 336
peace, 358
people pleasing, 346
perfection, 82, 140, 144, 312
perjury, 314
persistence, 13, 242
piety, 329
poison, 16, 40, 79, 93, 275
potential, 196
prayer, 162
prejudice, 256
preparedness, 223
present, the, 15
procrastination, 159, 297
progress, 81
prophecy, 149

propriety, 340
purpose, 72

R

rationalizing, 136
reality, 97, 110, 219, 318
recognition, 32
recovery, 17, 300
resentment, 204, 275
respect, 246
responsibility, 43, 63, 69, 124, 248, 279, 301, 333, 350
restraint, 39, 227
risk taking, 226

S

sacrifice, 217
sadness, 352
sanity, 6
sarcasm, 87
scripture, 3
self-deception, 10, 58, 66, 86, 111, 128, 178, 179, 186, 189, 210, 264, 288, 294
self-destructiveness, 56, 182, 192, 289, 321
self-esteem, 47, 89, 190, 236
self-knowledge, 232, 244
self-love, 138
self-pity, 255, 270
self-righteousness, 150, 222
selfishness, 220, 290
sincerity, 206
slavery, 141
sleep, 302
sobriety, 20, 49, 123, 219, 300, 339, 354
social drinking, 252
solitude, 221
suffering, 132

T

talent, 272
temperance, 5
temptation, 44, 100, 118, 171, 233, 235, 238, 268, 294, 347
thirst, 5
time, 351

toast, a, 2
trials, 327
truth, 23, 64, 139, 166, 249, 263

U
understanding, 213, 214

V
violence, 170

W
water, 208, 313
wellness, 109
willpower, 202
winning, 54
wit, 171
work, 154, 185
worry, 25